Humility
RE-CONTEMPLATED

Unveiling the Path to True
Freedom & Fullness of Life

Dear Antonia,

May the Lord bless you as you read this book. Enjoy!

Fr. Chimedu Enuh

30/12/2023

Humility
RE-CONTEMPLATED

Unveiling the Path to True Freedom & Fullness of Life

Chinedu Enuh

HUMILITY RE-CONTEMPLATED
Unveiling the Path to True Freedom & Fullness of Life

Copyright © 2023 by Chinedu Enuh

ISBN: 9798871846483

All Rights Reserved.

No part of this publication may be reproduced, distributed, or transmitted in any form or by any means, including photocopying, recording, or any other electronic or mechanical methods, without the prior written permission of the publisher, except in the case of brief quotations embodied in critical reviews and certain other noncommercial uses permitted by copyright law.

Cover Photo Credit: iStock.com/simoningate

Published by:
Gamechangers Media
Tel: +234 806 599 0019

To my parents, Mr & Mrs P. C. Enuh, who diligently raised me in the faith.

ACKNOWLEDGMENTS

"From Christ's fullness, we have all received grace upon grace" (Jn 1:16). Without God's help, we can do nothing (Jn 15:5). Therefore, I extend my heartfelt gratitude to God, who inspired and sustained this work to completion. To Him be all praise and glory.

I am also deeply thankful to everyone whose encouragement and critical reflections on the themes explored in this work served as sources of inspiration. Special appreciation goes to those involved in both the initial and final editorial processes, as well as those offering professional advice crucial to the completion of this project.

My profound thanks go to all of God's faithful individuals whose lives have profoundly influenced this work during my ministry to them. To you, I am immensely indebted. I express my gratitude to close friends and relatives for their moral support.

A very big thank you to my publisher, whose professional support proved invaluable.

TABLE OF CONTENTS

Dedication	v
Acknowledgements	vi
Foreword	x
How to Read this Book	xvi

Chapter One: Introduction — 1
"The Whole History of Faith is made of Humility…" — 3
What is Humility? — 4
Humility as Understood and Lived by St Vincent de Paul — 6
His descent and our "descent" — 7
Our Lords and Masters — 10
Humility and the Christian Meekness — 11
True Christian Understanding of Humility — 15
Why Does Humility Often Have a Negative Connotation? — 16

Chapter Two: The Transformative Power of Humility — 21
The Fount — 21
Humility: A Kenotic Experience — 21
When deeply wounded and stuck… — 22
Humus and Openness to the Transforming Power of God's Hands — 29

Chapter Three: Humility and the Sacrifice of Listening — 39

Humility and Listening — 39
Humility and the Obedience of Faith — 43
Humility: Breathing Life into our Daily Conversations — 49
A Samaritan Woman's Response — 58
Humility Opens the Door — 65
Get Out of the Way and Allow Grace — 65
Our Light in Darkness: Using Humility to Wait on the Lord — 67
…But not without the Risk of Offence — 73

Chapter Four: Humility and the Reversal of the Effect of the Fall — 77

Humility: A Weapon against the Vices of Jealousy and Envy — 78
Humility: Burning Down the Walls of Division Among Us — 80
Humility: A Decrease that Allows for the Divine Increase — 83

Chapter Five: Humility and the Christian Discernment of the Truth — 87

In Search of Truth — 87
Christian Discernment — 88
Presuppositions of Christian Discernment — 89
The Descent and Ascent of Humility in Discernment — 91

Chapter Six: Humility and Our Originality — 97

The Pressure of Authenticity Today — 97
Do Yourself a Favour and Be Humble — 101
Spiritual Lightness — 103
Humility, Truth, and Oneness with Oneself — 105
Humility and the True Love of Oneself — 107

Chapter Seven: Humility and Insecurity   109
Insecurity as a Universal Experience   109
Humility: A Tilled Soil for Authentic Christian Living 111
God's Word Tills the Soil of our Hearts   113

Chapter Eight: Humility and Being Aflame with God's Love   117
Humility and the Healing of Relationships   119
Humility and True love   121
An antidote to the Endemic Quest for Domination and Exploitation   123

Chapter Nine: The Courage and Fierceness of Humility   127
Humility as a Sign of Courage   127
The Fierceness of Humility   129
Living Authentically in Hope   130
The Irony and Scandal of Humility   133
Being Proud   134
Humility and the Christian Hope   136
Humility and the Human *Telos*   138

References   141

FOREWORD

During our seminary formation days, when discussing the virtue of humility, someone would inevitably collapse the conversation with a mischievous remark, "The only thing I'm proud of is my humility!" Towards the end of this most enlightening book on humility, Fr. Chinedu Enuh makes a similar statement but in a different and unambiguous tone when he says: "The humble are proud but proud of being humble."

Within the context of the entire book, this seemingly contradictory statement makes absolute sense. In our acute self-awareness, we realise that we are nothing without the God who gave us life, the One whom the author describes as elevating us from the dust of the earth and creating us in His own image and likeness (Genesis 2:7).

"It takes great humility to write a book on humility!" says the author. In fact, Fr. Enuh states in the opening pages: "Many would wonder how this man, in so much need of humility himself, could dare write a book on the subject." When he says, "Humiliation is part of humility," one feels he is revealing something of his life journey to date. He humbly often reveals the challenges he has faced in his lifetime and in the five years of his priestly ministry, especially in accompanying the homeless on their journey. The reader, I'm sure, will also feel reassured when he shares his moments of desolation and darkness.

Two keywords keep recurring in the book: "ascent" and "descent." We are introduced to a God who, in Jesus, made his humble descent among us. This is the God meant in Philippians 2:1-11, the God-man, Jesus, who did not cling to his equality with God but emptied Himself to become one of us, thus making our ascent possible – it is indeed the divine exchange.

In the annunciation to Mary, Fr. Enuh speaks of a double descent, that of God to become one of us and that of Mary, adopting the role of the lowly handmaid. In this double descent, says the author, is the ascent of all humankind assured. In this, our "true and original status is restored."

The ascent of humankind is possible only if there is an initial awareness of sin. The author cites the example of Adam and Eve. Their sin was a "false ascent," a "violent elevation," where the devil lured them to a false height. Quoting simply, Fr. Enuh further develops the human struggle to follow the path of righteousness: "What I want to do, said the saint, "I do not do; what I hate to do, I do" (Romans 7:19). St. Mark is also aware of that propensity to sin when he speaks of the evil which wells from within. (Mark 7:21-23).

This is a book of hope, a hope which promises eternal life for those who follow the part of humility, but it also offers hope in the present time. This hope is made possible for those who experience a sense of incompleteness in their lives by taking Christ as their model for daily living. Fr. Enuh takes as a key text the message of the Lord presenting Himself as a humble servant: "Learn from me," said Jesus, "for I am gentle and humble of heart" (Matthew 11:29).

St Vincent de Paul, founder of the Congregation of the Mission (Vincentians), and, of which Fr. Enuh is a member, models this life of humble servanthood, especially to the disempowered whom he considered his "Lords and Masters." His service to others is love in action – a love underpinned by humility. Quoting Pope Francis, the author says, "That if humility is absent, love has no access."

This book on humility is relevant to our present age, the age the author describes as having an "endemic quest for domination and exploitation." It is an age where truth is the antidote to all that is false. Two key texts from St John's gospel are quoted to illustrate the centrality and power of truth in the life of Jesus, a truth to which He later gave testimony when confronted by Pilate.

In John's gospel chapter 8, Jesus brings a more profound truth imbued with love and mercy to confront the truth of the law of the Pharisees as they brought their sense of justice to condemn a woman of sin. By exercising a deeper truth in humility and gentleness, the accusers were led to discover the truth of their own lives, and so, life and salvation were secured for the victim. The same truth is exercised in John's gospel chapter 4, where both Jesus and the Samaritan woman express a mutual expression of humility at the well – this truth, once more expressed firmly and humbly by both parties, brings understanding, conversion, and a new call to discipleship. In Fr. Enuh's words, both Jesus and the woman "walked the path of humble descent."

At the onset, Fr. Chinedu said that this was a book that could be shared in groups. It is ideal for guided reading or *Lectio Divina* groups (spiritual reading and reflection in common). In today's culture, one could envisage this book as an invaluable aid for community cell groups which aim to promote Christian values within a parish context. Each chapter is rich in scriptural references and contemporary insights. For each session, the group could take a chapter or a section of a chapter, each with an insightful sub-heading.

I feel privileged to write this foreword to Fr. Enuh's debut book. And may I ask the reader to be on the lookout for the counsel Fr. Enuh once received from his inner voice: "Chinedu, get out of the way and allow grace." Within these pages, you will find that the author has stepped aside while allowing you to be equally graced, whether reading alone or in your designated groups, those who, in humility, join you on your journey of faith.

Fr. Michael McCullagh c.m.
Author, *With Due Respect*

HOW TO READ THIS BOOK

This book is not meant to be devoured in one sitting. This isn't because you couldn't do so if you wished, but rather it has been intentionally structured as a guide for the purpose of revisiting and re-contemplating humility in various aspects of our lives. It has been thoughtfully divided into subheadings to encourage the reader to take the time to re-contemplate each heading in the context of their own life experiences. To draw an analogy, think of it like a tablet – one heading can be absorbed at a time, allowing sufficient time for contemplation, reflection, and digestion.

It is strongly recommended that each heading be actively engaged with, drawing upon the reader's personal life experiences. While the themes do not necessarily build upon each other, they collectively contribute to a richer understanding of the essence of humility. Each heading delves into an aspect of humility that can be contemplated independently of the others. The objective is to transition from merely reading and thinking about it to deeply contemplating the focal areas in the context of your life experiences.

Within your own life experiences, you will benefit most by seeking ways to put the reflected themes and ideas into practice, as humility thrives not in mere thoughts but in actions. While it's acknowledged that some themes are quite extensive, small groups, reading partners can reap rewards by engaging one theme at a time, allowing time for meditation, idea sharing, and praying for guidance and assistance from God.

Chapter 1

INTRODUCTION

Jesus says, "Learn from me; for I am gentle and humble in heart"
(Matthew 11:29)

Humility is truth, or rather, walking in the truth, and infinitely expresses itself in charity. It is not simply an idea or a feeling, but an action driven solely by and made alive in Charity. Its pure form is found in God, in whom, by participation, we hope to lead a life of humility. Humility can and should be a constant but ecstatic self-abasement by the power of his grace.[1] I hope to expound upon this wonder of humility in this book.

Today, there is no doubt about the sad reality that the virtue of humility has fallen victim to suspicion, not only outside but inside the Church. It is now hardly considered and/or frowned upon for its artificially negative and cowardly connotations. I cannot, nor intend to, exhaust here the reasons for this unfortunate situation. However, I seek to highlight some key ideas that can aid the re-contemplation and rediscovery of the beauty of humility. Various aspects of human life are contemplated here in the light of humility (set out in the various sections) to show how this virtue enlightens and is foundational to the Christian faith and human flourishing.

In this work, I invite you to journey with me in a re-contemplation of the virtue of humility, an invitation that requires some humbleness from both the invitee and the inviter. We all need humility, and this book will increase our awareness of that need. Presumably, you have picked it up for your awareness of our need for it, which is a good sign. My goal is to encourage the search for a deeper understanding and practice of humility and how this can be discerned.

Recently, I shared with a priest friend that I was writing a book on humility. And I clearly remember feeling unworthy to even say I was reflecting on that theme, let alone writing on it. I told him I was sure many would wonder how this man in so much need of humility himself could dare write a book on the subject. But right about then I felt these words spoken to me: "What you write would be a fruit of your many failures, weaknesses, and the little triumphs grace has accomplished in you. I want you to write about it because now you know the difference. Besides, you are simply an instrument in my hands."

Only then did I become courageous enough to start discussing this work with people. What I wish to emphasise here is that I am not perfect, nor have I attained my own humility goals. But I had to resist the subtle but dangerous pride of not writing on this specific theme as led. I am by no means an expert in the practice of humility, as I considerably fall short of where God would have loved me to be. Hence, this book is particularly an invitation to me who would also read it. More so, this work may provoke more questions than answers for us both, and I can only be grateful to God for the opportunity to look ourselves in the mirror of his grace.

By sheer providence, I once decided to revisit a book I had read with a friend in my seminary days. We would usually read spiritual books over the phone, share our thoughts and insights with each other, and then pray together. As I reread the book, I began to discover, or should I say rediscover, in a more profound way, the centrality and indispensability of the virtue of humility in a Christian's faith. I was reminded of how humility can help if we are to make sense of the story of our salvation and what God has done in us through his Son, Jesus Christ.

My initial plan was to 'retrace' the word humility, exploring how, if at all, its meaning has evolved over time. But then I decided not to focus on the historical development of the virtue of humility but rather to content myself only with its meaning, source, and centrality in the Christian life. As I contemplated whether or not to start immediately, I penned down a few thoughts, kicking off with some profound statements in Pope Francis's homily of Monday, 8 April 2013 at the Domus Sanctae Martha. As it were, those words became like, as you would say, putting new wood or coal in the fire. I felt sure that this was a clear signal to explore this theme, firstly for myself, and maybe for anyone the Lord may wish to speak to through this work.

"The Whole History of Faith is made of Humility..."

In the said homily, Pope Francis submitted that, "The whole history of faith is made of humility and speaks of humility to us all." He said, "Humility is Jesus' humility which ends up on the cross and is the Golden rule for Christians.... there is no other path. Unless I humble myself, unless you humble yourself, you are not Christians."[2] Towards the end of the homily, and perhaps to clarify what humility might mean lest it be misconstrued, he added, "I think we should say 'lowering ourselves.'" And then summed everything up, "If humility is absent, love has no access."

With those words, Pope Francis invited his audience to pray for a humble spirit. And confronted with and provoked by the truth that "unless I humble myself, I am not a Christian," and the fact that "if humility is absent, love has no access," I felt a fire in my veins that impelled me to reflect more on this all-important virtue.

So, for Pope Francis, 'lowliness' as a virtue isn't optional for a Christian. If "humility is Jesus' humility that ends up on the cross" and if "we are to conform ourselves to Jesus" (Phil 2:5), then our humility will gracefully lead us to the 'cross.' If the cross symbolises to a Christian 'Love in its perfection,' and humility 'leads us to the cross,' then humility can rightly be said to grant us access to love. Consequently, humility becomes the platform upon which love can thrive.

But what exactly is humility? What does it consist of? Who or what decides what humility is? Where does it come from?

What is Humility?

While it is in God that we live and move and have our being (Acts 17:28), he also fills all things (Ephesians 1:23). God, however, remains completely the "Other," an otherness that often frustrates many who set out to bridge this perceived gap in their bid to bring God closer to humanity. But the more an attempt is made to bridge this perceived gap, the more God's otherness becomes obvious. And this can be uncomfortable for those who, for good reasons, try to save God from being a distanced Being. Paradoxically, it is precisely in God's otherness that he can stay close and be present to us in ways that none other could. Psalm 112:4-6 captures this paradox, praying:

High above the nations is the Lord, above the heavens his glory. Who is like the Lord, our God, who has risen on high to his throne yet stoops from the heights to look down, to look down upon heaven and earth?

For the psalmist, it is a wonder that the Lord could stoop down to minister to us from such a height. This is natural to God, even though he is high above all things. Every instance of his relationship with his creatures is, in its very nature, an act of humility. Contrarily, due to our wounded nature, this descent is unnatural to us and impossible for us if unaided by grace. This is why God is the fount of humility.

To become more like God and rediscover a sure way to heaven, humility, I suggest, should be redeemed in our time, and brought to the centre of our lives. Pope Benedict XVI calls humility "the way of God." By that, he meant that each of God's actions is an act of humility, an articulation that is an aspect of divine revelation. He seeks to describe and make sense of God's self-revelation in Christ Jesus, with the aim of leading God's people to the imitation of Christ, becoming like him, as "the last of all and the servant of all" (see Mt 23:11, Mk 9:35). Pope Benedict XVI contrasted our way with what he had called "God's way," and said that "we, who are little, desire to appear great, to be first; while God, who is truly great, is not afraid to humble himself, and make himself last."

Etymologically, humility derives from *humus*, a Latin word that simply means the earth beneath. It seems to be interchangeable with the word for dust as in the case of the creation account, "for from the dust of the earth the Lord God fashioned man." While saying humility is good in itself, only God's grace gives it its particular character, making it transformative and life-giving. And when driven by charity, humility becomes attractive and should be highly desired for its potential to empower.

Humility as Understood and Lived by St Vincent de Paul

I intentionally dedicated this section to exploring St. Vincent de Paul's view on humility for many reasons. The main reason is that I am Vincentian myself, and during my formation came to appreciate the great Saint's thoughts on humility and his practice of the same. I think this work would be incredibly impoverished without St Vincent's thoughts on humility, which he practiced to the extent that some people thought he was quite odd.[4]

A good start would be to look at who St Vincent de Paul was. He was born on 24 April 1581 into a humble family in the village of Pouy near Dax in Southern Gascony, very close to the Pyrenees in France. Arguably, his initial intention to become a priest was mainly or partly driven by the quest for career advancement, to help the family. I imagine this attitude towards the priesthood would have been typical of his time, a difficult one. After he was finally ordained a priest in 1600, the Lord would use the events of his life to purify his intentions. This purification would lead to a deeper renunciation of self and start of his quest for ecclesiastical advancement and privileges. His life was not without unpleasant experiences that impelled him to rely on God alone for vindication.

One of those unpleasant experiences would be when he was wrongly accused of stealing. He had to endure shame and humiliation until his vindication. Another instance that drew him closer to God and purified his intentions more profoundly was his crisis of faith. He was once invited to pray for a priest who was unwell and whose crisis of faith had prevented him from being able to pray. In fact, the priest was on the verge of suicide when St Vincent visited him. Moved with compassion, Vincent asked God to transfer the priest's burden to himself.

What a radical sense of humility to choose to decrease that the other might increase! Anyway, the Lord heard his prayer, and the priest almost immediately recovered his peace of mind. From then on, Vincent struggled with his faith for some time. This continued until he finally made a firm and selfless resolve to follow Jesus Christ more closely in his mission and service to the poor. It was only then that this cloud of doubt and crisis of faith was lifted off him. Another incident that helped shape Vincent would be his quick removal as the Parish Priest of Clichy.

In all of this, what was evident in St Vincent's life was the gentleness with which the Lord guided his steps and drew him deeper to the path of humility and self-abasement for the sake and with the benefit of charity towards the neediest.

Among the groups he founded was the Congregation of the Mission ("Little Company," as he called it) in 1625. This is a group of priests and brothers who live in a community for the service of people who are poor. Vincent also co-founded the Daughters of Charity with a noble widow Louise de Marillac in 1733. This is a group of women whose mission is to serve, as above of whom he tells his brothers and sisters that they are 'our Lord and Masters.' While this confession (the poor are our Lord and Masters) might sound simple, it was revolutionary at the time because the practice of it was and remained a radical witness to the incarnation. Consequently, St Vincent is the Patron saint of charitable works.

His descent and our "descent"

What you will read here is simply my interpretation and understanding of St Vincent's thoughts on humility in case you find them inconsistent with what you may have heard about this great Saint.

Owing to Vincent's false intention to ascend in his ecclesiastical career, the Lord gently redirected him through difficult experiences. Thus, he freely promised to commit his whole life to the service of people who are poor should the Lord grant him freedom from his spiritual ordeal. St Vincent then turned away from a false preoccupation with his career. He no longer considered the humble path of the poor as optional but as a necessary Christian path. So, for him, humility is not optional but a fundamental Christian virtue. No wonder Pope Francis firmly said, "Without humility, you are not Christians."

For St Vincent, humility is central to the message of the truth that Jesus came to reveal and teach. Therefore, in the second chapter, paragraph 6, of the Common Rules of the Congregation of the Mission, St Vincent talks about humility as self-abasement for charity's sake. While quoting scripture, he says:

Learn from me, for I am meek and humble of heart. By it we are reminded, as he himself affirms, that the earth is possessed through meekness because, by the exercise of this virtue, men's hearts are well disposed to be turned back to the Lord, something which is not accomplished by those who deal harshly and roughly with the neighbour. Moreover, heaven is acquired by humility, for the love of self-abasement is wont to raise us up, leading us step by step from virtue to virtue, until we all arrive at our goal.[5]

St Vincent seems to have highlighted from the above excerpt the decision to pursue humility if we are to attain the goal set before us and for which we have been captured by the Lord (Phil. 3:12). Hence, he says that heaven is acquired by humility. The "descent" required and enabled by humility sets and fixes our gaze on the upward calling of the Saint. Pride does just the opposite. Falsely lifted up, pride fixes our gaze on the worthless things of this world, and as such, we are constantly weighed down.

Humility, for St Vincent, is the "foundation of evangelical perfection and the core of the spiritual life" (CR II, 7). In one of his conferences, he wondered why only a few people practise this foundational and decisive virtue of humility. At the same time, he gives an answer and says:

It is because it is ravishing to speculate on, but its practice is disagreeable to nature; its very appearance is disagreeable to nature. Practising it means we should always choose the lowest place, put ourselves below others, even the least, bear with calumnies, seek after contempt, love abjection; and to all these things we are naturally adverse. Yet we must overcome this repugnance; each of us needs to make strong efforts to arrive at the actual exercise of this virtue. Otherwise, we shall never acquire it.[6]

St Vincent's description of humility challenges me due to the gap between my current daily life and what the virtue of humility summons me to. However, I was encouraged to hear that it is mainly acquired by practice (similar to other virtues, like courage).

Concerning humility, unless I intentionally choose and practice to take a lower place or even the lowest place, I will never attain humility. As much as humility is a gift and a grace, it cannot actualise itself in me unless I work on it; "Grace perfects nature," says St Thomas Aquinas. And as I engage in the spiritual exercise of training myself to be humble, the grace of God thrives in me, making my little and sincere efforts very fruitful. Furthermore, and in fact, only in humility are we made worthy of doing God's work.

Humility for St Vincent is simply the truth, while pride is the opposite, namely a lie. Being the truth then, he considered it as a powerful weapon that conquers the devil and his snares. It follows that, to become instruments of conversion of souls, we must be accompanied by the grace and the practice of humility to attract hearts to Jesus and not to ourselves. It follows that "humility is the origin of all the good that we do."[7]

In his book, *The Way of Vincent de Paul: Contemporary Spirituality in the Service of the Poor*, Fr. Robert Maloney, CM, presents, as it were, a contemporary understanding of this invaluable virtue of humility, and describes it as:

A recognition of our creatureliness and our redeemedness, both being gifts of God's love... we are completely dependent on God, there is nothing we have that we have not received... Humility is gratitude for gifts... It involves a servant attitude.[8]

Maloney shows that the virtue of humility is what leads to a Christian's gratitude. In recognition of the truth that we have indeed received all we have and will ever have, we are more eager to give up our very selves in our loving service to God who is present among us, in the persons of people affected by poverty whom St Vincent called 'our Lords and Masters.' Though worshipping the Lord is our dutiful and joyful service, we now approach the throne of mercy in adoration and thanksgiving.

Our Lords and Masters

It takes profound humility not just to call people who are poor 'our Lords and Masters,' but, perhaps, more importantly, to serve them as true Lords and Masters. When people who are poor, vulnerable, or needy approach us, say the homeless person who may not have washed their body for a while, it takes profound humility to see through the way things appear and see Christ in them. When I started working as a chaplain with a certain charity organisation for homeless people, I sometimes struggled with seeing beyond some homeless people's challenging behaviour. I had to remind myself of St Vincent's words, "They are our Lords and Masters."

It becomes even more difficult when you are dealing with people who are going through serious substance misuse, PTSD, and other serious challenges that make it difficult for them to conform to what we would consider acceptable social norms and behaviour. To serve people like this, a great deal of self-abasement is required if our services aren't going to simply be another service with a sense of duty and not with intense gratitude and a recognition of the utter privilege afforded in serving them. St Vincent was very clear about this. He often advised his two little companies on how to serve sick and people who are poor with respect and honour. But as many other saints, such as St Francis of Assisi and St Mother Teresa of Calcutta, have reflected upon, this is impossible without God's grace.

Humility and the Christian Meekness

Humility and meekness are often used interchangeably by some because of their closeness. But they are nonetheless different in their inner character. We shall closely consider how Jesus used meekness to guarantee a future inheritance. I argue that the virtue of humility underpins meekness and, if practised, will enable us to practise meekness as Jesus encouraged.

We read the Sermon on the Mount in the Gospel of Matthew and hear Jesus say, "Blessed are the meek, for they shall inherit the land (earth)." *Blessed* comes from the Latin word (noun) *Beatitudo*, which is rendered as *happy* or *blessed* in English. This explains why some biblical translations would simply use *happy* to point to the *telos* (end), which was to be fulfilled in Jesus, which ancient Israel's hope anticipated, the moment of complete fulfilment of all hopes and divine promises.

However, Jesus' use of the words *blessed* or *happy* here cannot be confined only to the future. It is a part of the spiritual reality of the believer, acknowledging within "the present moment" that they are already blessed. They should be happy for this future reality that is constantly breaking into the present. Although, of course, this can only be fully realised in the fullness of time, when God becomes all in all, and we see him not as in a mirror but as he really is, and all tears are wiped away (1 Jn. 3:2, Rev 21:4).

But what was it about meekness that made Jesus associate such a huge promise with it: a promise to inherit the earth or the land (which suggests a promise of perpetuity). Let us consider the meaning and use of the word *meek* in scripture. The Greek words *praus* (adjective) and *prautes* (noun) were often used in the scripture, particularly in the Gospel of Matthew and some epistles of Saints James, Peter, and Paul. I started this work by quoting Matthew 11:29, "Learn from me; for I am gentle and humble in heart." The reason is that some translations use gentle instead of meek, even though there is a different Greek word for gentleness, which refers more to the outward action, and meekness would most often refer to an inward disposition or action or response. So, you find that the word *praus* is often translated to mean either gentle or meek.

Aside from these minor translation issues, let us consider how the words *praus* or *prautes* were used. Margaret Mowczko traced an early use of this word to Xenophon (c. 430-354 BC), who lived centuries before the New Testament was written. He was an Athenian Military leader, historian, and Philosopher. He wrote two treatises on the art of horsemanship in Ancient Greek and not in *Koine* Greek in which the New Testament was originally written. According to Mowczko, Xenophon used the word *praus* in reference to animals to mean: firstly, gentle training of horses; secondly, taming a growling sheepdog, taming of fish; thirdly, about amiability between soldiers and warhorses. She then concludes that the word *praus* can be translated into English as "most gentle, soothing, to calm down/be calm, gentle, to tame and move reasonably/ more quietly."

Moreover, Mowczko argued that meekness in this sense is not likened to weakness, as evident in how the word was used in the New Testament to mean a gentle, mild, or regulated temper. For the Christian, meekness, like humility, submissiveness, and self-restraint, are positive virtues. They are about putting aside or relinquishing power in relationships. It is the antithesis of arrogance, uncontrolled anger, and aggression.[9] Being an antithesis to these negative emotions, it is empowering since it frees one from them. Corollary to the above, we can immediately see the connectedness between meekness and humility, as they are both fruits of Christ-like character made possible by the power and grace of the Holy Spirit. Through meekness, Christians can live in freedom by regulating anger and controlling their temper in the context of a relationship and other life situations. To do this, humility plays a significant role in how we see ourselves and others and where we have placed our reward, especially regarding relinquishing power as Christ did in his relationship with us and the Father (see Philippians 2).

Jesus was wounded and humiliated. However, through his meekness, the bible says, in what we now call the 'suffering servant hymn' (Isaiah 53), *"he was despised and rejected, a man of sorrow, acquainted with grief, despised, wounded and bruised for our transgressions and iniquities...like a lamb that is led to the slaughter, and like a sheep that before his shearers is dumb, SO HE OPENED NOT HIS MOUTH."*

This suffering servant hymn points to Jesus' life, passion, and death. In it, we see a radical manifestation of meekness to which every Christian is called to live daily. Jesus was clearly offended to a limit that no one has ever been. Yet he restrained himself and lived before his Father in freedom.

This recalls St Vincent de Paul's thoughts on the power of meekness. Obviously, as a man of the 17th century, he spoke of meekness in the language of his time. But the profound wisdom with which he described the importance of these virtues still shines brightly today. He describes meekness as the ability to handle anger by suppressing or expressing it. But in the end, its expression or suppression has to be governed by love (XII 186, XII 187, and XII 188). In this way, the Christian remains approachable, affable, and serene, especially in countenance, regardless of the situation (XII, 189).

As we clearly see in the suffering servant's hymn of Isaiah 53, St Vincent thought that:

Meekness makes us not only to excuse the affronts and injustices we receive, but even inclines us to treat with gentleness those from whom we receive them, by means of kind words, and should they go so far as to abuse us and even strike us on the other face, it makes us endure all for God. Such are the effects produced by this virtue. Yes, as a servant of God who truly possesses it, when violent hands are laid upon him, he offers to the divine goodness this rough treatment and remains in peace"(XII, 192).

As is very typical of St Vincent, he spoke in simple and clear language. He also thought that meekness disposes people to turn to the Lord (CR II, 6).[10]

Meekness turns us to the Lord since it makes us conform to him. Through meekness, we constantly walk in the descending path of humility, on whose wings we mount, especially when offended and are naturally provoked to anger. Put differently, with meekness, we can "chew before we swallow." In provocation, we can hold our tongues, and calm down before acting or speaking. But the truth is this: the arrogant cannot be meek because the latter is the antithesis of the former. Hence, humility is the foundation upon which the virtue of meekness thrives and is practised.

True Christian Understanding of Humility

Scripture presents Jesus as the One in whom we can find and learn the true meaning of humility (see Mt 11:29). St Paul in Phil 2:5 invites us to have the same mind that was in Christ Jesus. This is the mindset of humility, one that is infinitely charitable and of a charity that is infinitely humble in a way that is beyond the reach of human strength. Drawing from Jesus' *kenosis* (self-emptying) in Philippians 2, we begin to see that humility is the complete giving of ourselves in service to the other as an offering to God. It is a "descent" whose 'end' is solely charity. Unfortunately, this is rarely uncontaminated in us, at least not without any expectation of reward (e.g., success, fame, attention, approval, acceptance, applause, competition, financial or even simply to feel good about ourselves or our spiritual growth). This is to do with the woundedness of humanity from Original Sin.

Do not be shocked when I say humility should not be lived simply with an intention fixed on our spiritual growth. Although it is a righteous thing to pursue one's spiritual growth, charity insulates our humility so that it does not become selfish, with 'self' ('I') as the *telos*. Love is not self-seeking but simply rejoices in the truth (1 Cor 13:5-6). True humility must flow from, impelled, sustained by, and directed towards charity as its end. Only then can it resemble what Jesus meant when he said, "Learn from me, for I am humble in heart."

Why Does Humility Often Have a Negative Connotation?

Most definitions of humility would present its nature as having to do with the sin of pride. This is not true, as it pertains to God who is the source and embodiment of humility. It is only true regarding us human beings, and this is due to our woundedness. But if humility was taken to always have something to do with sin, it then follows that Jesus' words in Matthew 11, "Learn from me; for I am gentle and humble in heart," would suggest that Jesus had some inherent falsehood or sin from which he tried to humble himself. But then we know that Jesus never gave in to pride (see Jn. 14:30), neither did he ever seek vain glory (Jn. 8:50), nor was he ever an attention and fame seeker that he should humble himself (Jn. 6:15). He did not even try to 'cling to his equality with God' (Phil 2).

So, there must be an understanding of humility that Jesus had in mind when he said, "Learn from me, for I am humble in heart." Some have tried to solve this problem, and I here argue that humility is not necessarily about turning away from sin. They would argue that humility is simply accepting our true self, who we are before God and others. While acknowledging that this is a huge step forward, at the same time, it immediately begs the question, how do we get to the point where we know who we truly are? Secondly, what do we do with this knowledge of our true self when we know and accept it? We are to remember that Jesus, knowing that he is God, did not cling to his equality with God but emptied himself (Phil 2:6). Yes, we should know and accept who we truly are. But humility does not consist simply in knowing but in being. It is an action, as I explained at the beginning.

Humility transcends the simple act of knowing who we are. More importantly, it consists in not clinging to that which we have come to know that we are. Thus, it is rightly seen as self-abasement driven by charity, but for the service of others. "Though he was in the form of God, Jesus did not count equality with God a thing to be grasped but emptied himself."[11] When we look at the Eucharist, what we see is God's deliberate self-abasement, the deliberate vulnerability of the Mighty One, the condescension of the Divine Majesty, yet, from this self-abasement issued the glory and power that saved and saves us.

St Paul leaves the reader in no doubt that humility is much more than simply knowing one's true identity, which is very important. St Paul drew from Jesus' life and pushes this further to show that having understood and accepted our true identity, if we are to know what we are self-abasing from, we are then, for the sake of charity alone, impelled to let go or instead live as though we are not, even though we are. Jesus, even though he was God, lived as though he was not (as a human being in all things but sin). We who are not God ignorantly and strangely sometimes live as though we are God; hence, thinking of ourselves more than we ought to do (see Rm. 12:3).

Let us return to the nature of humility as lived in Jesus. In Him, we see humility in its purest form, one that isn't about sin and the negation of self. Jesus is God, and God is Love. Therefore, all his actions are acts of love and humility. This revelation of humility, as action, flows from his eternal, true state. And indeed, humility in this state in God is interchangeable with truth.

Although we strive to lead a humble life with sincerity of heart, our experience of humility will always be a descent from a "false" state. In the words of Cardinal Raniero Cantalamessa, "We lower ourselves only from a false or pseudo-height, a height to which we were unlawfully elevated by pride, vanity, anger, and so forth." We elevate ourselves due to our woundedness. Cantalamessa also thought humility is always a negative virtue for human persons "because it condemns our base instinct to elevate ourselves above our neighbours."[12]

So, given our wounded humanity, humility becomes a virtue that breaks down our falsely elevated heights and gets us grounded in reality, the truth of who we truly are: interconnected and linked as we are as the Body of Christ and, therefore, ideally, servants to one another. "Complete my joy by being like-minded… Do nothing out of selfish ambition or empty pride, but in humility consider others more important than yourselves" (Phil 2:2). We can therefore say that humility presents as a descent because where we were, wasn't real in the first place. But what we perceive as descent is actually an ascent because right in our descent from our false-pseudo height is our true Christian ascent or elevation.

Jesus addresses this in the Gospel of Luke 22:27 – about greatness. He says to the people, "The greatest among you should be like the youngest, and the one who leads like the one who serves. For who is greater, the one who reclines at the table or the one who serves? Is it not the one who reclines? But I am among you as the one who serves." This is clearly a divine invitation to the hard truth that the world's descent is indeed the Christian's ascent, and vice versa. Thus, Jesus completely changes our contemporary understanding of humility and calls us to learn from him. This is the way to happiness, peace, and holiness of life, without which we will lack true Christian joy and fulfilment.

Once this truth is grasped, humility, at least, becomes attractive again. It becomes true advancement; as Pope Francis says, "…advancing for Christians means lowering of oneself."[13]

Chapter 2

THE TRANSFORMATIVE POWER OF HUMILITY

The Fount

To not misconstrue the virtue of humility, which is a*ction (actio)* expressed in love for another, we must quickly, without delay, turn to and fix our gaze on Jesus Christ. God is the unfathomable fount of humility, as His essence is constantly, 'ecstatically,' and unreservedly self-giving. Therefore, every action of God towards His creatures, right from creation to eternity, is by its very nature an act of humility.

However, all this was not clearly seen and understood until its pure revelation in Jesus Christ. Jesus is the revelation of God as humility, which is both action and a person. For God so loved the world that he sent his only begotten Son Jesus Christ (see John 3:16), and since in Him (Jesus) all the fullness of the Godhead (divinity) is pleased to dwell (see Colossians 2:9), one can say that in this action God gives Himself.

Humility: A Kenotic Experience

God's humility is reflected in all His actions towards his creatures. He delights in stooping down to what He has created. And this movement towards the other is what George A.

Maloney, SJ, describes as "the ecstasy (ek-stasis) of standing outside of or beyond the self-control of oneself in order to move towards others in self-giving"[14] The humbler we become, the more we become like God, increasingly and freely moving towards the other in love. Because God is infinitely humble, He infinitely 'enjoys' the ecstatic movement toward others. Except in medical conditions and other factors we cannot address here, humility releases us from the heaviness and shackles of pride and falsehood. Falsehood makes us isolate, withdraw, and go into ourselves, but humility, through self-emptying, frees and releases us. We, therefore, become lighter to freely move towards others in charity.

Consequently, this kenotic experience of humility draws us closer to Jesus' experience of freedom, which He hinted at in the Gospel of John when he said, "For the prince of this world is coming. He has no hold over me"[15] The virtue of humility allows the Holy Spirit to uproot the stronghold of pride and falsehood, which are practically lies. As these strongholds, which often accumulate over time during our lives, are uprooted, we become truer to ourselves, and thus freer to move towards the other with a living authenticity – an ecstatic experience of humility, which is the truth of who we really are before God. For this, and as wholly accepted, loved, and protected children, we are not afraid to move toward others in self-giving love.

When Deeply Wounded and Stuck...

One of the things that have become quite clear to me, especially since my ordination to the priesthood, is the reality of Christian struggles. Perhaps this is because the priesthood grants the priest a rare and unmerited privilege of sharing in people's deepest experiences. With faith in God, the faithful often entrust their deepest struggles to the priest, who *in persona Christi* receives and offers them up to the Lord.

The faithful often confide in the priest about their stuck and stagnant situations. In my pastoral experience, as I listen to them, I usually can see a soul awaiting divine justice for years and has continued to wait, only that there is no strength to wait anymore; like the Bible says, "Hope deferred makes the heart sick, but desire fulfilled is a tree of life."[16] I can almost feel the sickness of the heart, not necessarily of any biological illness but of weariness from waiting. Some would tell me that they feel abandoned or, at the very least, ignored by God. I remember listening to a man who said, "Even my earthly parents wouldn't ignore me this long."

As such, everything is at stake when a Christian's situation reaches the depth of feeling abandoned. Often, with that feeling comes a sense of orphanhood, making one question who they really are to God. Accordingly, purpose and meaning, which flow from knowing who we really are, become lost. Unfortunately, this is the situation of many sitting on church pews, waiting and hoping to hear a word of peace or hope, which is why I think the homily is both a privilege and an opportunity for the priest to abandon himself in God's hands as a living instrument and channel of divine oracle, so that, by grace, God might speak to His flock, ministering to each of their hearts.

Thus, the homily should not be a time to show off or share personal preferences to the flock, as beautiful as those might appear. Instead, it should be borne out of prayerful reflection. It should be seen as a moment to be treasured and never treated casually or directed towards preferred activities like praises or 'other' prayer sessions. I have found that it is indeed a privilege to have a moment of encounter with the Lord, Christ the Head, who speaks to His people. It should not degenerate into a flex of theological prowess, as seated right there are souls expectant of a consoling encounter.

Anyway, back to the point I was trying to make… I remember hearing a young man say, "Father, I feel lost, wounded, and broken, and I don't know what to do." Probing further, I was shocked and wondered how he could even hold on that long in faith. Some will say, "Father, I have lost faith and trust, and I don't think there is any need to wait anymore. If only God could give me a tiny sign to encourage me to continue waiting." One could tell it wasn't just that their prayers weren't being answered, as even more severe is the fact that they feel God is not doing enough to encourage them to keep waiting.

Usually, as a priest, I would journey with them in those moments of doubt, disappointment, and abandonment, reassuring them that it has never been heard that God abandoned anyone, as it is not in His nature. He is called Emmanuel because He is always with us. But then, as you hold them before God in prayer, you can begin to feel the heaviness of the burdens of these faithful people, who, more often than not, simply come to see if they can find strength or encouragement in what now seems like a never-ending wait.

This scary reality has often driven me to pray while waiting for a 'living word' capable of restoring hope. Certainly, there have been many testimonies and experiences of God's goodness and divine interventions, but the point here is that many people still feel stuck and helpless due to the endemic nature of their problems. I have often felt helpless, especially when I could not offer the help I believed they needed. As is often the case, words in such circumstances often feel inadequate and simply repeat what one must have previously said.

So, the question is, what is the place of humility here? How can we be talking about humility with someone whose life experiences have brought them so low to the ground that, in their understanding, there is nothing left to abase oneself from? Even in a situation like this, humility can establish one on the firm foundation of the truth, and thus bring about a lifting up. Scripture says, "The LORD upholds all who fall and lifts up all who are bowed down."[17]

As chaplain to an organisation that supports many homeless clients with substance misuse problems, I can say I gained a lot of insight into addictive behaviour, something I had little or no knowledge of before. There is a sense in which I can liken the feeling of some of the faithful who feel stuck to the feeling of those clients, who often cry and are filled with fear because of their situation. I remember speaking with a client who, at the time, had made so much progress in overcoming his substance misuse problems. Now, the *Passage* had found an accommodation for him to view before he signed a contract and moved in. He was excited about this, and I could sense it from his tone as we chatted away in the dining area. He kept repeating, "I can't wait to see the place, move in, and sort out my life." As our chat progressed, he said this to me: "I have made huge progress. I have worked on myself and been clean from drugs for months. However, I am afraid." When I asked why he was afraid, he said, "It has happened before. I always start off well but end up very badly. I am afraid it is going to happen again. I know it's going to happen again. It is like a circle. But I am just going to do my best."

As he spoke, I could feel his fears, one that melted my heart. I encouraged him and promised to pray for him if he didn't mind. "Oh no, I don't mind! I would really appreciate that," he had said. This would probably be the experience of many, especially those with extreme addictions and substance misuse problems: that feeling of being trapped. And when sober, one clearly sees the place or person he/she ought to be, which now seems unattainable. We remember who we were but remain trapped in a web of addictive and destructive behaviour. Yet, to our knowledge, we are doing our best, given the circumstances. As it were, we have exhausted all our options, are tired, and are hoping that something could change this time. I remember a client once saying, "I clearly know what I should be doing, but I am not doing it, or rather, can't do it. Why I can't do it is what I really need help in understanding." That is an honest and sincere search for the truth and shows humility.

God remains with me even when my senses fail

In all these, one senses that feeling of being stuck and exhausted while waiting for a solution. Even when all hope is gone, there usually seems to be a remnant that keeps one in that place where he or she simply feels helpless and abandoned by God. God may now appear either as a saviour who cannot save me or a God who cannot feel my pain, thus stretching me beyond my limits. Unfortunately, when ignored, we feel bereft of God's intervention. Therefore, after a long period of feeling this way, we start entertaining the thought of being abandoned by the Lord. (As the client had said, "Even my own dad would not have taken this long.")

In this situation, every step becomes a huge hurdle. I feel

everyone is getting along well, and I am lost. If only God could, at this point, give me just a little light of encouragement by way of some progress or improvement in my struggles, I would be content. But nothing is happening as far as I can see, feel and know.

Still, amid all this, God's word says that He is always with me and will never leave me alone. He tells me that his name is Emmanuel (Isaiah 7:14), a mighty saviour (Zephaniah 3:17), my present help in time of need (Psalm 46:1-2), and the One who would never allow me to sink beneath the waves nor be consumed by the fire of life (Isaiah 43). Though my senses fail me now, as I can no longer feel His consolation, presence, or intervention, faith summons me to submit humbly to these truths even though I seemingly cannot receive or be saved as I would have loved to be right here and now.

In this way, we unite with the One who has truly felt what we are feeling right now and cried out in a loud voice on the cross, "My God, my God, why have you forsaken me."[18] In these words, Jesus identifies with every human experience of estrangement, abandonment, being stuck, and helplessness. But then Jesus will not go on crying aloud in these words. What he then does next is what humility invites us to do when feeling lost and abandoned. Jesus utters a prayer of submission and says, "Father, into your hands I commend my spirit."[19] Likewise, we should submit to the Father's will as Christ did and was, in the end, glorified.

In this submission, we often start to see what God is doing, even in what seemed like the arid land of our lives. This self-committal is the acceptance and total resignation to God's will in whatever form it appears, even when it might seem unfair, unjust, and even, most times, wicked and ungodly. The Christian does this knowing that God, the Beloved, is worth everything, including our lives, as it pertains to His will and plans for us. It takes humility to see another person (God) as deserving more than you do. Moreover, humility is needed to self-commit one's life into the hands of God, simply to do as He wishes.

The Christian may have been struggling with one or a series of addictions for a long time and now feels overpowered by these behavioural patterns. They may be desperate to overcome these but see little or no progress. It might be worth approaching God with grateful hearts for our other blessings or progress in other areas of our lives. Often, our desire for huge outcomes could blind us from seeing the tiny, decisive, grace-filled, and grace-powered progress we make daily. Truth be told, most of our lives are made up of these often so-called seemingly insignificant acts of grace. Without "knowledge" of these, we will get exhausted waiting.

Therefore, to see these tiny actions of grace, which we call progress, the Christian must move in the descending direction and desire to be humble like Jesus. Progress may not always be measured by one's expectations and desires, but perhaps on the mustard seed principle of God's kingdom. These tiny actions of grace might look small, but that is all it takes to become or grow into the great tree of the kingdom that will serve as a shade for many (Mark 4:31-32). This descent would require not comparing oneself to others. The Christian should not compare their present with their past or future dreams. They should instead content themselves in gratitude with the present, gently abandoning themselves into God's hands as they look into the future.

Humus and Openness to the Transforming Power of God's Hands

Humility, in a living way, puts one in God's hands for transformation, while pride does just the opposite. The hands of the Lord are not so high up there that we should fly up to place ourselves in them—they are lowly placed. Therefore, only in lowliness can one consciously put himself or herself in God's hands. "For he looks upon the lowliness of his servant."[20] This is what the Blessed Virgin Mary prophesied in the Magnificat. Once placed in God's lowly hands (in the sense that God is humble in all his ways, at least in the revelation of Himself to us), transformation by grace becomes inevitable. We often assume the loftiness of God's hands, which affects how we seek to reach out to Him.

I always love to reflect on the dramatic experiences and prayers of the tax collector and the Pharisee in the temple. St. Luke's gospel dramatically contrasts the two to offer a common ground upon which we must stand to approach God. St. Luke hinted at this at the beginning of that parable and says, "To some who were confident of their own righteousness and looked down on everyone else, Jesus told this parable."[21] From this preamble, it immediately becomes clear to the reader that some people are about to be brought down from their high horses of false righteousness, and, even more seriously, to reveal their shocking ignorance. Then it continues,

"Jesus told this parable: Two men went up to the temple to pray, one a Pharisee and the other a tax collector. The Pharisee stood by himself and prayed: 'God, I thank you that I am not like other people—robbers, evildoers, adulterers—or even like this tax collector. I fast twice a week and give a tenth of all I get.' But the tax collector stood at a distance. He

would not even look up to heaven but beat his breast and said, 'God, have mercy on me, a sinner.' I tell you that this man, rather than the other, went home justified before God. For all those who exalt themselves will be humbled, and those who humble themselves will be exalted."

With this parable, Jesus reveals the truth about righteousness and humility. Righteousness is impossible without humility because humility places us in God's hands as a sacrifice. It is from this sacrifice that the Lord makes of us that righteousness flows. The Christian is aware that righteousness is of the Lord, not us. Even with our good and righteous deeds, it must be said that it is still God's gratuitous grace through the one and all-sufficient sacrifice of Jesus Christ by which the Lord makes us holy. Deductively, the word sacrifice comes from two Latin words, *sacra* (holy) and *facere* (to make or to do), which, when put together (*sacra-facere*) would mean to "make holy."

The Pharisee had got it wrong thinking his perfect obedience to the commandments could let him claim merit before God. This is an attitude that, in the end, makes God a debtor to our merits. Rather, these became merits only because the Lord had made our works and deeds meritorious. Therefore, our boasting is based on grace and not on our works.[22] The former places the merit on God, while the latter tends to place the merit on the Christian. No wonder the Scripture says, "For it is by grace you have been saved through faith, and this is not from yourselves; it is the gift of God, not by works so that no one can boast."[23] In the final analysis, it is in God's mercy that we trust, even with all our good works.

Am I now watering down the importance of good deeds? God forbid! Certainly, our faith would be dead without good deeds;

our good deeds, faithfulness, and obedience to God's commands are like seeds we sow to reap their fruits. The same is true about disobedience and sin. However, the Christian who does not recognise that mercy is their hope is yet to understand the nature of what was accomplished in Christ and in what state humanity would have been had it not been for His mercy made manifest.

Anyway, the Pharisee comes to God with his own merits instead of God's merit. Based on that, he demands God's attention as reward for his goodness. He seemed to have forgotten that unless aided by grace human actions and righteousness are filthy rags before God. "We have all become like one who is unclean, and all our righteous deeds are like a filthy cloth. Like the wind, we all fade like a leaf, and our iniquities take us away."[24] In these words, Isaiah reminds the people of their present state. Due to sin, God's people had been through a lot at the hands of their enemies. As it were, this prophecy of Isaiah reminds the people how deep their wounded nature was, to the extent that even their supposed righteous deeds were simply abominable before God.

That's how far humanity is steeped in hopelessness without God's mercy, which was to be revealed in Christ. Hence, God's people were left with only one choice, especially after the difficult lesson of the devastating effects of sin, which they had learned from their exile experiences. That choice is God's mercy, for which Isaiah immediately appealed and said, "But now, O Lord, You are our Father; we are the clay, and You are the potter; we are all the work of Your hand."[25] What a humble prayer! What a truth upon which alone God's people can stand and approach God!

Unaided by Grace, We Are Incapable of Righteousness

Drawing from the experience of ancient Israel, there is a sense in which we can say that humanity, unaided by grace and mercy, remains simply incapable of righteousness. And if it is of God's grace and mercy, would it not be ignorant and rude to boast of it while looking down on others? This is a false height. Thus, the Scripture reveals that the Pharisee approached in falsehood and, consequently, left without being favourably heard, for he had prayed to himself. In other words, he was brought low, even though, in his mind, he may have fooled himself into thinking he approached God in prayer.

In contrast, the tax collector, very mindful of his sins, stood afar, beat his breast in penitence, and appealed to God's mercy, which in the final analysis counts even after we have rightly done all our works. "So, likewise, when you have done all those things that you are commanded, say, 'We are unprofitable servants. We have done what it was our duty to do.'"[26] The exact words of the tax collector were, "God, have mercy on me, a sinner." Yes, he recognised the truth about his state, that he was a sinner, perhaps a grievous one. He approached God based on this truth but with hope in God's mercy. His self-abasement was accompanied and aided by hope in God's mercy. Consequently, he attained a privileged state of humility, automatically placing him in God's faithful hands. And as Jesus tells us in John's gospel, "Whoever comes to me, I shall not turn away."[27] Having placed himself in God's transforming hands through humility (truth), we are told he went home justified, "For all those who exalt themselves will be humbled, and those who humble themselves will be exalted."[28]

It might be unpleasant to acknowledge and act in response to the truth in us. We might even feel ashamed of and unwilling to identify with this truth. But here is the point: just like the dust of the earth was transformed in God's hands and we were created, our lives are transformed if we are willing and open to allow God to touch our humble state.

Thus, humility places us, like the biblical dust of the earth, in God's hands for transformation, fruitfulness, and purpose. I will return later to the relationship between humility and purpose, or the discovery of one's purpose through humility. But I want to add here an extract from a brief exhortation I gave some time ago on the power of grace to transform the dust of the earth. I would like to do this because humility, which is self-abasement, can often present as meaningless, shameful, and, in fact, like what the image of the dust often represented in the Scripture. But then, we should remember what the scriptures have revealed about the power of God's grace to raise from the dust, transform, and bring out something precious even from such a seemingly meaningless state.

The Exhortation: The Power of Grace to Raise from the Dust

Right from the beginning of the creation account, we see the power of grace to raise and transform from the dust, or rather, to create from the dust. Genesis 2:7 and 1:27 tell us that out of the dust of the ground, God formed man in his own image; male and female, he created them and breathed into his nostrils the breath of life. He became a living being. Here I am combining the two creation accounts to bring out, more beautifully, the power of grace in touching and raising one from the dust of our situations. This is not to say that we were dust before God transformed us into human beings. No, not at all! However, the creation account reveals, among other things, that our creation is a revelation of the power of grace that can reach down to the insignificant (such as dust) to bring out meaning, purpose, and something as beautiful as the human person.

Dust in the Old Testament

We would better appreciate what I am saying once we consider closely the Old Testament understanding of dust and its significance. The image of dust is often used to symbolise suffering (see Micah 7:17, Gen 3:14—licking the dust like a serpent). Something unwanted, of no value, and trampled underfoot. Although dust is itself a creature, it can often denote nothingness, shame (see Lam 3:29), helplessness, or weakness, as Ps 103:14 prayed that God may remember how weak we are since we are dust, etc. In other words, dust isn't something anyone desires. Hence, Isaiah 52:2 talks about shaking off the dust of sin, shame, and guilt. 'To return to dust,' as we find in Gen 3:19, would mean to experience death. Yet from this very dust, the Scripture tells us that God created something as beautiful, the human person, in his own image, and destined him to a life of grace and eternal life.

Now, here is the point: the dust of the ground, from where God formed man, would have remained dust had it not been touched by the hands of grace. The moment the hands of grace held it up, the story changed. In Jesus' life, death, and resurrection, God has perfectly taken up every aspect of humanity because Jesus is the grace that makes salvation possible. Hence, a transformative change is already taking place in us, especially in our lowly state.

Humility Places Us in God's Hands

While humility does not make us void of purpose and meaning, it nonetheless places us in God's hands like the dust of the earth for a divine transformation. God is humble. Thus, he is the foundation upon which all else stands. Speaking to the Church in Corinth, St. Paul tells them that Jesus is the foundation upon which all will be built.[29] The Christian is invited to build on this foundation, not with silver or gold but with their lives. A foundation is rooted in the ground, and you can only build on a foundation if you are in touch with it. So, to build on the eternal foundation, Jesus, means firstly, a descent, being in touch with the foundation, and then becoming one with it. In laying down our lives on the foundation, we become one with it, unnoticed, just like the foundation of a building.

I am neither a builder nor do I have an interest in construction but have seen and admire beautiful edifices and structures. Often, when you travel to some of the big cities in Europe, you will see many tourists jostling to take pictures of iconic buildings; you see them lost in ecstasy as they admire them. My concern here is that, throughout my years of travelling, including a year-long experience in Italy, I don't remember seeing an admirer of a building talking about its foundation as something beautiful. Often, the focus is on the body of the building rather than on the foundation, which, in the first place, isn't visible in most cases. Imagine a tourist standing next to the Houses of Parliament in London and saying, "O goodness! See how beautiful the foundation of the Houses of Parliament is. Isn't it beautiful?" I guess doubt the sanity of the fellow. You can't help but wonder what could be beautiful about the 'buried' foundations.

Moreover, the truth is this: the foundation is there but hidden. Although the perceived physical structure can say something about the foundation, the foundation remains hidden, at least in most cases, even though the entire edifice rests on it. To a non-architect or non-builder admirer, the foundation is entirely insignificant, rarely remembered, and adds nothing to the perceived beauty of the structure. Yet, in the order and scheme of things, the foundation is indeed foundational, without which no other perceived beauty could stand. Indeed, it takes the eyes of a professional to see the foundation, even though it is hidden away under the ground.

Humility Keeps One Closer to the Foundation

Humility draws us closer to the foundation, making us one with it so we can become almost unnoticed. But in the hiddenness that comes with humility, we are placed in God's hands, where every meaning, purpose, and beauty lie. The Christian who has placed his or herself in God's hands through self-abasement and descent of humility will not be void of purpose, meaning, and beauty. However, this may need to be clarified in a way or with a purpose that the world can understand. Just like the casual eyes of a non-professional could not, from the apparent physical structure, see the beauty of the foundation buried in the ground, even so the world is unable to appreciate the beauty of the Eternal Foundation and those who, through humility, are closely attached to it.

Placed in God's hands through conscious self-abasement, we are in touch with the foundation of all things and are in cooperation with grace. Through genuine self-giving, our lives also serve as foundations to comfort others in their times of need and vulnerability. Since humility brings us closer to the eternal foundation through descent, humility makes us conform more closely to Jesus. Humility gets you grounded in reality and truth (Jesus is the true foundation) and makes you stable (you are grounded and based on a firm foundation). Humility provides a context within which every other virtue and spiritual exercise can thrive and bear fruit. It is transformative and life-changing for you when you practise it. "Learn from me; for I am gentle and humble in heart."[30] Being insignificant and meaningless according to world standards would not trouble you if you understood in whose hands you have been placed and the transformation that He brings from your making the descent of humility.

Chapter 3

HUMILITY AND THE SACRIFICE OF LISTENING

Humility and Listening

While listening is very sacrificial, humility is a must-have virtue for the Christian who wants to be a better listener. In other words, a good listener is a humble person, and vice versa. I often hear people talk about being good listeners and how important that is to the person being listened to, but rarely do we emphasise the link between the ability to listen to others for their sake and the ability to humble oneself.

Matter-of-factly, you can't hear others if you haven't heard yourself. And to do that is to be aware of oneself and the promptings within. It is often the case that we are unable to hear each other because of an interior chaos or noise or the ignorance of one's voice. Humility as a virtue, as already established, grounds Christians in the truth about themselves, about God, and about the created order. Only on the basis of this truth can we be present to a soul to listen and, please God, understand. From a false height, the Christian is deaf even to his or her true voice crying for authenticity, let alone the voice of the other. To truly listen requires a sacrificial descent, which turns Christians away from themselves to the other with the openness of loving, self-gifting hearts.

I used a 'loving, self-gifting heart' because of its resonance with selflessness. The soul moves towards the other simply for the sake of the other. It is not to defend or present oneself as a good listener, not even with only the intention of providing a solution or knowing what to say, but primarily to listen with attentiveness. Humility is helpful here because it enables the listener to accept that what is at stake here is not the listener and his ego, or prestige, but the good of the other. In a sense, true and good listening often entails self-denial. The listened-to is placed first and at the centre of attention. The listener comes second. You can see why it is sacrificial.

This sacrificial descent prevents us from being distracted from focusing on the listened. Honestly, I am sometimes also distracted in listening to the faithful, especially when I am exhausted, still have a lot to do, or allow 'self' to get in the way. Now, I fully realise what my then spiritual director used to say to me: "You can do your work only if you are well. Take care of yourself, else you won't be of any use to anyone." Truth be told, if you don't listen to yourself, you can't listen to another. However, humility is needed to avoid slipping into self-indulgence all in the name of listening to oneself, in which case the self is brought to the centre of the art of listening, distorting the whole process.

Listening to Hear the Lord

The divine invitation to listen attentively to others does not require us to think about our response and, or crucially, a solution. True or good listening is not a competition to be paranoid, compulsive, or anxious about what to say to the person listened to. The Christian's response is most likely to be 'carnal,' prompted by head knowledge, if they fail to listen deeply and attentively due to impatience or pride. Often, the listener comes under self-imposed pressure from their perceived expectations. "I am supposed to know what to say. I should have the answer to these problems. I should be able to make this person better in the end." While all these worries can be sincere, they can become distractions from the most important thing: to truly and attentively listen. Humility helps us to see that we are not the providers of solutions or healers, but the Lord is.

You may have all the reasonable expectations for all you want, but what matters in the end is what the Lord says. But how can I know what the Lord says if I am busy thinking about Bible verses to quote or a theological text to use while ignoring the living encounter of listening to the one who speaks through the soul before me? No theological idea can ever outweigh the supreme privilege of being able to listen attentively to God. Just be still and listen: "Be still and know that I am God."

When not listened to...

Personally, I have had many experiences when I felt I was not listened to because the responses I got came off as automated responses and seemed to satisfy the supposed listener rather than myself who needed to be satisfied. I remember going to a familiar counsellor once to share something I was struggling with. At that time, I was already a deacon, yet struggling a bit with my confidence, as is often the case at that formative stage. I went to this counsellor who I thought had professional listening skills. After I shared my challenges with him, he completely ignored what I shared and started commenting on my accent, pronunciation, and other unnecessary stuff. Initially, I thought he was distracted, so I repeated my dilemma to him, this time expecting a more tailored response. Instead, he went harder on the English accent pronunciation point. And referring to one of the days he heard me read in public, he said, "I couldn't understand what you read." With more exaggeration, he went on and on about how I should improve my English accent.

Don't get me wrong. This is not a criticism of the counsellor. I also see nothing wrong with a professional advising a client on such matters. But what was strange was the context. Was I shocked? Yes, I was. Did I feel better after that? No, I felt worse. Did I feel listened to? Not really, as what I heard was simply a preset, something he possibly already made up his mind to say to me someday since he first heard me speak. Did I think it was intentional? No, he probably thought he listened to me very well.

I feel 'the self' got in the way. The sacrificial descent of humility could have helped him give up his mission of speaking to me about my English accent and focus on addressing the actual reason I was there. The listened-to would have been placed first, at the centre of attention, to encounter him. The Christian who tries to listen from a lofty height of presumption (obviously a false height) will always be deaf, not just to the soul before them but also to oneself. From a lofty false height, it becomes about what one needs to tell the person listened to than about what the listened to needs to be told.

If that counsellor had listened to himself, he probably would have heard himself and dealt well with those out-of-place responses—even if it meant admitting to not knowing what to say. Humility makes it possible to carefully and lovingly accept one's ignorance of a particular truth. We must not always have something to say, as some listening encounters come to us to keep us in that place of accepting our limitations and then knowing that we are not the source of what the souls before us need. Thus, we urgently and humbly turn to God in prayer.

Humility and the Obedience of Faith

You may have noticed that whenever we struggle with the virtue of humility, obedience to God's word becomes an unbearable and meaningless burden, and we immediately seek to compromise and water it down to suit ourselves. Hence, we refuse to accept the word of God for what it really is (see 1 Thess 2:14) and treat it as mere human words.

"Faith is the assurance of things hoped for and the conviction of things not seen" (see Hebrews 11:1). The Catechism of the Catholic Church tells us that "it is a supernatural gift that enables us to believe whatever God has said, a personal adherence to God and to the whole truth he has revealed (and I would clarify here that it includes the whole truth he has revealed about Himself, us, and you).[31] It is a grace (CCC 153) and the beginning of Eternal Life (CCC 163). He who believes has eternal life.

However, this faith invites us to the obedience of faith in every aspect of our lives, in our actions, words, prayer, relationships, conversations, thoughts. As described by the catechism, the obedience of faith is "a complete submission of one's intellect and will to God."[32] It is the 'obedience of faith' that ensures that our faith is alive, active, and fruitful.

The word *obedience* is from two Latin words, *ob* and *audire,* which literally mean to "listen thoroughly." This is not just hearing, as in the case of hearing the sound of a car, but a conscious turning away from oneself to the speaker. This turning away from self to the other, to whom we must pay attention, therefore, becomes a form of sacrifice, openness, and a decision to humble oneself. When you see a person who finds it difficult to listen with full attention, you have seen someone who finds it difficult to be obedient. When you find a person who is quicker to speak than to listen, then you are most probably looking at someone who is not patient in true obedience.

Obedience, therefore, requires listening, and listening requires humility:

"Hear, O Israel, the Lord our God is one Lord; and you shall love the Lord your God with all your heart, and with all your soul, and with all your might. And these words, which I command you this day shall be upon your heart, and you shall teach them diligently to your children..." (Deut. 6:4-9)

As faith comes through hearing and hearing the word of God, obedience comes by listening deeply with humility. Only through humble listening can one be patient, especially when there is a considerable gap between the expectation of the Gospel and what the Christian perceives as a possible Christian response. The gospel will always call us to obedience at a height way above the limits of human strength. But it does not expect us to attain this height by pretending to be what we are not, or by forcefully trying to elevate ourselves in order to attain what can often be a lofty call of the gospel. However, it is only attainable by our cooperation with grace.

True obedience to God flows from the Christian's acknowledgement of their humanity with all its limitations and apparent gap between where one is and ought to be. They first incline and lean on the breast of the Redeemer to listen carefully to His heartbeat. Here we hold on to the truth that the Lord knows better and cannot ask us for what He cannot accomplish in us by His grace. Secondly, the Christian then sets out to act according to God's will and command despite all its challenges. They do this knowing that it is right and just to obey the Lord, for indeed He is deserving of all our praise, respect, and adoration.

Humility helps us to wilfully submit our intellect to God, not being wise in our own understanding, eyes or wisdom (see Prov. 3:7).

Sin Thrives in the Absence of Humility

Sin thrives more in the absence of humility. We often shy away from the word sin as if it has become non-existent, with some even getting upset whenever a preacher mentions sin. Understandably, this reaction typically flows from experiences with preachers who, in the past, preached only about sin and nothing else. As it were, they made the whole Christian life about avoiding sin. Sadly, this occasioned the panic that today is caused by the mention of sin. Yet, sin is a reality everyone experiences and deals with. Why must it then be a problem to talk about our lived experience? Therefore, pretending that sin doesn't exist is not the solution. Instead, a healthy approach, like Jesus did in his time, is the way forward. In the light of God's mercy, therefore, I wish to speak about sin (which is disobedience to God) and how humility aids us in triumphing over many sins.

The Catechism of the Catholic Church (CCC) begins the section on sin by placing sin and mercy together. In this way, mercy becomes the context within which we deal with our sin, so not to despair in our frailties. This is what it says:

1846 "The Gospel is the revelation in Jesus Christ of God's mercy to sinners. The angel announced to Joseph: "You shall call his name Jesus, for he will save his people from their sins." The same is true of the Eucharist, the sacrament of redemption: "This is my blood of the covenant, which is poured out for many for the forgiveness of sins."

1847 "God created us without us: but he did not will to save us without us." To receive his mercy, we must admit our faults. "If we say we have no sin, we deceive ourselves, and the truth is not in us. If we confess our sins, he is faithful and just, and will forgive our sins and cleanse us from all unrighteousness."

1848 As St. Paul affirms, "Where sin increased, grace abounded all the more." But to do its work, grace must uncover sin so as to convert our hearts and bestow on us "righteousness to eternal life through Jesus Christ our Lord." Like a physician who probes the wound before treating it, God, by his word and by his Spirit, casts a living light on sin: Conversion requires convincing of sin; it includes the interior judgement of conscience, and this, being a proof of the action of the Spirit of truth in man's inmost being, becomes at the same time the start of a new grant of grace and love: "Receive the Holy Spirit." Thus, in this "convincing concerning sin", we discover a double gift: the gift of the truth of conscience and the gift of the certainty of redemption. The Spirit of Truth is the Consoler.

It then goes on to explain what seems like the character of sin, which, to me, suggests a great absence of humility:

1849 Sin is an offence against reason, truth, and right conscience; it is a failure in genuine love for God and neighbour caused by a perverse attachment to certain goods. It wounds the nature of man and injures human solidarity. It has been defined as "an utterance, a deed, or a desire contrary to the eternal law.

1850 Sin is an offence against God: "Against you, you alone, have I sinned and done that which is evil in your sight." Sin sets itself against

God's love for us and turns our hearts away from it. Like the first sin, it is disobedience, a revolt against God through the will to become "like gods," knowing and determining good and evil. Sin is thus "love of oneself even to the contempt of God." In this proud self-exaltation, sin is diametrically opposed to the obedience of Jesus, which achieves our salvation.

1851 It is precisely in the Passion, when the mercy of Christ is about to vanquish it, that sin most clearly manifests its violence and its many forms: unbelief, murderous hatred, shunning and mockery by the leaders and the people, Pilate's cowardice and the cruelty of the soldiers, Judas' betrayal - so bitter to Jesus, Peter's denial, and the disciples' flight. However, at the very hour of darkness, the hour of the prince of this world, the sacrifice of Christ secretly becomes the source from which the forgiveness of our sins will pour forth inexhaustibly."

Sin, from the above excerpt from the Catechism of the Catholic Church, is presented as a violent self-elevation against God, either in word, deed, thought, or desire. One cannot do violence to a person to whom you have humbled yourself for the sake of charity.

When we see what is happening in our world, especially in the churches, we can perceive a subtle but violent self-elevation of her members against God. We now think we know more than God and His words and principles, which many now judge to have outlived their usefulness. Today, we tend to have moved away from obedience to God's word to making the word of God obedient to us.

Of course, this is not to say that the gospel shouldn't be preached within the context of people's cultures and ways of thinking. What I am saying is that in whatever way the gospel is preached and responded to in our time and in ages to come, obedience of faith to God's word remains different from obedience to religious designs and inventiveness. There is nothing wrong with change and inventiveness because love itself is infinitely inventive, as St. Vincent de Paul thought. Change can be a great gift as we read the signs of the time and respond to God's words within the life events of our time. In fact, this is one of the reasons for this publication.

However, this desire for change shouldn't be our mere invention. It should always be in response to God's word in our lives events in our own time. Unless we keep this in mind, change and inventiveness would drive the inventors and initiators to insanity, making it about them and their preferences. My religious and liturgical preferences cannot give life nor satisfy the desire of the faithful. Instead, all our changes and inventiveness should align with God's will and in obedience to His word. But then, obedience requires the humble acknowledgement that you are not the master in God's business. You are and indeed should be proud to be called an unprofitable servant, a steward whose approval, reward, and punishment lie in his master's (Jesus') hands.

Humility is, therefore, needed to keep us sane in the face of the changes and inventiveness of the Holy Spirit because it places God at the centre, not you or anyone else. Only God can be at the centre and remain sane since it is His place. When humility is absent or frowned upon, the self comes to the centre, and consequently, disobedience becomes the order of the day and the standard.

Humility: Breathing Life into Our Daily Conversations

When you go on the street or even in the Church, you immediately notice an apparent but often unexpressed frustration about how difficult a genuine and free conversation is increasingly becoming. One tends to wonder why this is the case. Most people want to talk and be listened to, they want to leverage the rights to speak and be heard. But the problem arises when they are confronted by the direct consequence of those rights, which necessarily demands the responsibility to accept that the other has the same rights as they do. Conversation presupposes understanding; when the former is absent, you cannot say a conversation has genuinely occurred.

At the heart of the frustration I mentioned earlier is the undue focus on making oneself understood rather than on understanding the other person. There is an unintended asymmetrical expectation and presumption in that. Contrary to what conversation is for, most people try to dominate and control the discussion. The downside of this is that everyone is left feeling unheard. Consequently, civil unrest, violence, and the breakdown of relationships happen. We are often not willing to pay the price of a genuine and truth-based conversation, upon which depends the peaceful co-existence of different people with different views and understandings.

Jesus Christ is a great, unique conversationalist. Although He could be hard, firm, upfront, and straight in his conversations, He nonetheless was always open to entering into a tender, loving, and lively conversation with the people, no matter how difficult the situation was. He always wished to have a genuine conversation with the people, especially with the Scribes and Pharisees, who often approached Him with preconceived ideas of who He was and certainly with the vicious intent of trapping and thus condemning Him. We immediately see the people's impatience and rejection to hear and understand him. An example of this would be Jesus' encounter with the religious leaders of His time in John 8 and many other discourses in the gospels.

Possibility of Offence if it is True and Healthy

Let's look closely at that discourse because we could learn much there. Perhaps, I should say this now. While we would always want to have a peaceful, offence-free conversation, we all know that true conversion does not necessarily mean the absence of offence or disagreement. The attempt to remove every possibility of offence in all conversations produces people incapable of pursuing the truth and being truthful to each other in love. Every conversation is, in some sense, a pursuit of the truth. And in the quest for truth, we risk offending each other, though unintentionally and sometimes in a profound way. Humility helps us to bear what often looks like a sharp and deep cut by opposing views while respectfully making our case known to the other. It takes humility to be truthful, especially when it is known that this would lead to a painful response, which could be anything ranging from standing alone, being abandoned, and then to a verbal and physical attack, humiliation, shaming, and cancellation.

The eighth chapter of St. John's gospel begins with Jesus coming from the Mount of Olives to the temple, and as the people were drawn to him, He sat down and began to teach. This will be the context of the controversial but truth-based discourse that followed. The discourse begins with Jesus being tested by the

Scribes and Pharisees. They brought to Him a woman of whom they made a public spectacle and claimed she had been caught committing adultery. Then they said, "...and Moses has ordered us in the law to condemn women like this to death by stoning. What have you to say?" Quickly, the Evangelist revealed the intention of the Scribes and Pharisees, saying, "They asked Him this as a test, looking for something to use against Him." Jesus knew that it was a test that could cost Him His life if He stood against what the holy Moses taught and gave as a law. We then were told that, as Jesus wrote on the ground, they persisted with their questions, thus revealing how aggressive, forceful, and harassing falsehood can often be in a conversation.

Likewise, today, in our daily conversations, falsehood tries to intimidate or bully the truth with its populist loudness. More often than not, the innocent and the weak are overcome by these voices, which they sometimes end up identifying as theirs whilst they are not. And with these colour groups' aggressively mounting pressure on the innocent, standing by the truth in a conversation could appear like a matter of life or death. Constrained by conscience, though, the innocent must now 'take on or confront' the inevitable consequences of standing by and speaking the truth. Are you going to make your conversations truth-based or rather fruits of your submission to the bully of falsehood, which unfortunately and strangely enough appears very compassionate and sometimes pious (devout), as we find in the gospel of John 8?

When Conversation Begins to Fail, We Listen Deeply

Often, when an intelligent conversation begins to fail, instead of the parties involved humbly and patiently listening deeply, both or one begins to bully the other with what I call 'narcissistic compassion.' It has nothing to do with the search for the truth but has everything to do with resentment, a vicious thirst for vendetta, and the humiliation of the other. That's when you may hear things like, "How dare you say such an insensitive thing to me or about them...? You are insulting; show some compassion. You are not acknowledging my subjective feelings." Now, you quickly find that what is meant to be a mature conversation becomes an attack on the person. This vicious blackmail could range from simple phrases like, 'show compassion,' and then to the extreme situation of cancelling the person simply for disagreeing with seemingly compassionate ideas that have absolutely nothing to do with the pursuit of the truth.

In this situation, the Christian must be aware of this reality but must also manifest the courage of humility, remain grounded on the firm foundation of the truth, and thus be open to the challenge of an adventure in the pursuit of truth. Unfortunately, what we often read in the Scripture between Jesus and the religious leaders of his time was a hardness of heart towards the adventure of the pursuit of the truth, which is what, in most parts, our conversations are about.

The Scribes and Pharisees came with closed hearts to speak with Jesus in John 8. They had already pre-empted the options for Him. Either He agreed with us, and this woman gets stoned to death, or He renounces Moses' teaching, which would merit Him the death penalty. Either way, Jesus was about to be discredited as a true messenger of God. So, something very vicious was going on there; the identity of Jesus was in dispute. In other words, the truth, which is the salvation of all people, was indeed at stake.

Would Jesus fall for that? Not at all! Jesus would get them to think about the truth in all of these, perhaps not in the ways they had expected. John tells us that Jesus bent down and wrote on the ground. Of course, they persisted. Then, Jesus stood up and called them to the heart of the matter. Jesus knew quite well that they were against Him, the truth, His reputation, and eventually His life. But He must count all those things as nothing (Phil 2) and focus on the crux of the moment, which is the salvation of their souls. This is what humility does in a conversation: it removes the self, to a great extent, from the centre of the conversation. Therefore, even the most difficult conversation becomes life-giving with the truth as the goal.

Being the Light of the world (Jn. 1), Jesus will now powerfully speak to the individual person's heart in a way that pierces through and beyond any religious camouflage and vicious mob or group. He says, "Let anyone among you who is without sin be the first to throw a stone at her" (Jn. 8:8). With this, Jesus called them down from their high horses, and they all went away one by one. Why? This is because they were irresistibly led to face the truth about themselves and their salvation. Were they offended? Perhaps, yes. Was Jesus' statement polite at this point? Yes. But was the truth sacrificed at the altar of politeness? No. The darkness of that group identity, which was bound in lies, was dispelled, and they saw themselves for who they truly were in their words and actions. Ultimately, the woman was set free and granted a fresh start.

However, the rays of this light did not stop there. From verse 12, Jesus, as it were, radically turned up its brightness and zoomed in very closely to the truth to lead his people to the saving truth. In verse 12, Jesus says, "I am the light of the word. Whoever follows me will never walk in darkness but will have the light of life" (Jn. 8:12). As you would expect, the Pharisees, with their closed hearts, were unwilling to seek understanding. Instead, they immediately accused Jesus, which they will continue to do for the rest of the discourse. Does this remind you of where we are in many societies today? What people do not understand, they vilify. If you say something that does not correspond to a specific pattern of thinking, you are called names and condemned. While this is often a well-calculated attempt to shut down the truth and enforce what could be seen as demonic conformity, it is nonetheless a mind-disturbing manifestation of ignorance.

'The Scandal of the Truth'

As we read on in the gospel, it might begin to appear as though Jesus was being too rigid and uncouth in His words. But in reality, we witness the scandal of the truth when one humbly but courageously endures all things to save or be saved.

Back to John 8, they accused Jesus of testifying on His behalf to invalidate His testimony. Jesus acknowledges this accusation and says, "Yes, I testify on my own behalf, and so does the Father who sent me; he testifies on my behalf" (Jn. 8:18). Perhaps, suspecting that He was calling God His Father, which would have been considered blasphemy within that culture at the time, they asked Jesus, "Who is your Father?" (Jn. 8:19). Mind you, this is not a question coming from a heart that genuinely seeks understanding. It was a question that sought reasons to judge and condemn.

Jesus was certainly not surprised by human ignorance and malicious intent. However, God wants us to acknowledge our ignorance so that we may indeed seek wisdom. Thus, the Bible says in James 1:5, "If any of you lacks wisdom, let him ask God, who gives generously to all without reproach, and it will be given you".

As the Scribes and Pharisees continued to lock their hearts against the saving truth, in verse 21, Jesus releases the full beam as it were and says, "I am going away, (referring to his death), and you will search for me, but you will die in your sin. Where I am going, you cannot come." With these words, Jesus pointed to Himself as the only way to salvation; of course, they were utterly lost. At this point, Jesus restrained Himself and said in verse 26, "I have much to say about you and much to condemn, but the one who sent me is true, and I declare to the world what I have heard from him." This is quite an interesting verse because Jesus clarifies that He had a lot more to say and possibly to condemn. But then He declared only what He had heard from the One who sent Him: the truth. Here, we could see courage and love to witness to the truth that saves the people, and the humility to submit to the Father's will, Our God who is Truth (Jn. 8:26). Jesus' witnessing must be about the Father and His will (truth), otherwise, it becomes about Jesus.

Isn't this what happens to us in a conversation? Once a conversation becomes about me, my ego, prestige, and honour, then self-restraint flies out the window. The Christian then goes all the way to attack, bully, vilify, and dominate the conversation. When that happens, the conversation will no longer be about the truth. Hence, verse 31 says, "Jesus said to the Jews who had believed in him, if you continue in my word (by that he meant acting and saying only what we have heard from him as Jesus did with the Father), you are truly my disciples, and you will know the truth and the truth will make you free." Ignorantly, they thought that being descendants of Abraham was the same as being truly free. So, they asked why Jesus said they would be free. Jesus answers them, "If you were truly Abraham's children, you would do what Abraham did and not seek a way to kill me, a man who has told you the truth I heard from God."

As they insisted on their claim of being of God, Jesus tried to convince them that being of God isn't achieved by mere talks but by deeds that flow from listening to God's word. Then, it became apparent that they were not willing to listen. Hence, in verse 47, Jesus says, "The reason you do not hear them (God's words, which is what Jesus was speaking to them) is that you are not of God."

Again, perhaps if the Scribes and Pharisees hadn't made the conversation about themselves, they would have given a chance to the word of life being spoken to them. When the self is at the centre stage, pride blinds and deafens, and consequently, we get aggressive (passive or non-passive). No surprise then, in verse 48, they went all out and accused Jesus of being a Samaritan (godless) and of having a demon. This resistance to listening to Jesus will continue until verse 58, which hints at Jesus' identity as the ageless, "Before Abraham was, I am." On hearing this, they picked up stones to throw at him, but Jesus hid and went out of the temple (Jn. 8:59).

When the Place of Worship of the True God Lacks Truth

Interestingly, this was happening inside the temple, a supposed place of truth and worship of the one true God. The temple had become a place where lies thrived and truth bullied into a corner.

This was the temple where the light of truth should shine brightly, but there was Light being rejected. This was them preferring darkness and a conniving silence that had nothing to do with truth and compassion but everything to do with an insecure and falsely elevated self. Finally, in verse 59, the darkness could no longer hide due to the brightness of the light of the truth (Jn. 5:5). They then picked stones to throw at him, "but Jesus hid and went out of the temple."

Just imagine how many prophets have been bullied and forced into silence or hiding in our time. To a great extent, the rage of pride has rendered us incapable of having a real, truth-based conversation. We pray that in our conversations, the truth might not be forced out of its place. The Truth might hurt, but through love and meekness, we can journey together respectfully in the pursuit of the truth that sets us free. Do not be quick to call names and jump to conclusions when you do not understand. Enter a conversation with openness and an expectation to learn. You don't really know as much as you think you do. Wisdom should help us know this and be humbled by that truth. Also, honouring the present moment, God may have a reason for you to be in that conversation – divine providence has orchestrated your meeting and conversation with that particular person.

In the same vein, you are not as important as you think you are, even though you are worth more than you can ever imagine. By grace, you are worth the life of God because that is what it cost Jesus to save you. That's how much value Grace has placed on you. But do not forget that it is only by grace. Therefore, allow the source of this grace to be at the centre of your daily conversations, and we will start witnessing the truth as Jesus did.

Do Not Cast the Messenger Away!

Let us not cast away our prophets simply because their words are inconvenient to us. If the Christian journey and witnessing becomes entirely easy and the gospel stops challenging us and sometimes provoking us to think and act, then we are not getting it right. In the encounter with the word of God, like every honest and living dialogue, there is bound to be tension sometimes simply because it is accurate, living, and not automated. We must ask God for the grace of courage to engage with this life-changing adventure of the pursuit of the truth in our daily lives and conversations. For example, in the gymnasium, one knows he or she is getting it right if one continues to challenge oneself and not simply give in to comforts. So, in our daily conversations, let us push ourselves further on that path of humble descent, and we will find our conversations life-giving and exciting.

A Samaritan Woman's Response

A sharp contrast to the attitude of the Scribes and Pharisees in John 8 would be the response and disposition of the Samaritan woman at the well in John 4. I will quickly run through the conversation to contrast her response with the attitude of the Scribes and Pharisees in John 8. I acknowledge this is not a fair comparison since it would have been the duty of the Scribes and Pharisees to defend and protect the religious laws as the religious leaders of the people. So, there might have been reasons for them to be firmer and more suspicious of Jesus, a man they would have thought went around transgressing the religious laws of their fathers. But that's the interesting thing about the whole discourse. These leaders, who were meant to understand the workings of God, were utterly ignorant and blind to his ways. And the Samaritan woman, on the other hand, from the so-called pagan nation, Samaria, showed more openness to the pursuit of the truth. She had her doubts and questions, but she was not afraid to embark on the adventurous and uncertain journey of the pursuit of the truth.

Here, I won't be giving theological symbolisms of the time she came to the well and her previous five husbands. This will be a simple look at her openness met with Jesus' ever-openness to the noble exercise of the pursuit of truth.

The dialogue between Jesus and the Samaritan woman took place on the way, as Jesus travelled from Judaea to Galilee but had to pass through Samaria (Jn. 4:1). Firstly, we must immediately note that divine providence had orchestrated the discourse in a way that she was left alone with Jesus, whose disciples had gone to the city to buy food. In addition, the Samaritan woman came at noon, a time that scripture scholars thought was quite unusual for someone to come to draw water from a well. Perhaps this was a deliberate attempt by the woman to come at a quiet time when no one would be there. But in the end, it all worked out well.

Now, there she was, alone with this strange man (a Jew who sat next to Jacob's well). The Evangelist immediately tells us that Jesus sat there because he was "tired out by his journey" (Jn. 4:6). As the woman approached to draw water, Jesus said to her, "Give me a drink" (Jn. 4:7). There is a sense in which one could already see in Jesus a deep sense of humility. There is no doubt that Jesus knew what He was about and intended to do by taking the woman conversationally on a life-changing journey. But Jesus started by humbly exposing His own vulnerability, presenting Himself as the one in need. He engages with this woman, not from a lofty height as Christ and the Son of God, being God. Instead, Jesus stoops down. This is what I call the descent of humility.

When Humility Provokes

Jesus already knew the strife between the Jews and the Samaritans and how the latter were regarded as godless and consequently avoided and despised by the Jews at the time (see Matt 10:5-6). Jesus knew whom He was speaking to and how shocking and provoking His request to this woman would have been. But this apparent provocation by Jesus' humble request will serve as a trigger for what follows. However, Jesus' request was indeed a game changer since no Jew would 'condescend and risk' asking something from Samaritans. His request would have been a radically scandalous act for any devout Jew at the time. Honestly, it was a radical descent of humility. He is the one in need, asking for help and, as such, exposing to this woman His own vulnerability and need for her help.

Shocked and surprised, maybe provoked, the woman would have been confused. Who wouldn't be? Thus, she replied, "How is it that you, a Jew, ask a drink of me, a woman of Samaria?" The Evangelist exposes the gravity of Jesus' request and says: "Jews do not share things in common with Samaritans" (Jn. 4:9). Of course, Jesus knew all that, as I indicated above. But I want to draw your attention to Jesus' descent as an entrance into this life-changing discourse with her. Let us also pay attention to the woman's openness, even when Jesus tells her the hard truth and invites her to a deeper openness, as she boldly challenges Jesus' claim of being able to give living water. "If you knew the gift of God, and who it is that is saying to you, give me a drink, you would have asked him, and he would have given you living water" (Jn. 4:11).

I could not help but imagine the woman looking at Jesus from head to toe and wondering if he was okay. But then she said, "Sir, you have no bucket, and the well is deep. Where do you get that living water?" Often, in our conversations, we have to confront some negative perceptions that appear in ways that can distract from the onward journey of the pursuit of the truth. Obviously, this woman already had a few reasons to walk away from this stranger:

1. He was a Jew, a people who vowed never to have anything to do with us.
2. It is a lonely time of day to be engaging with a male stranger.
3. He could be dangerous; perhaps he is not mentally okay.

He hasn't got any buckets, yet he claimed to be able to give living water. Besides, what does he mean by living water?

When Humility Courageously, but Respectfully Speaks the Truth

Despite all these reasons, the woman respectfully makes her case with her sheer quest for understanding. She may have needed clarification, but she was not in a haste to conclude, make assumptions, or call names as we would do today. Courageously, she continued to engage in this noble cause, the pursuit of the truth. Thus, she says, "Are you greater than our ancestor Jacob, who gave us the well and, with his children and flocks, drank from it?" Obviously, you could sense the tension here. Certainly, both were not yet on the same page, but they remained open to each other; neither pride nor self is at the centre here. You would remember that the entrance to this conversation was Jesus' humble descent. I do not doubt that if we try as often as possible to enter into our daily conversations with humility, we will be able to rescue free speech, defend the truth, and live a more fulfilled life. The path might not be easy, perhaps, often littered with tensions and the danger of offending each other, but God's grace is made available. And recall that without humility, love has no access.

The Risk of Offence

As you read this account, you could not help but see how Jesus risked offending this woman in the pursuit of the truth. You could also see how the Samaritan woman, though with great respect for Jesus, still risked offending Him, especially when, as it were, she said yes to Jesus, "Who do you think you are? What makes you think that you could ever offer me any water that would be of more value than the one our ancestors gave us?" This is a revelation of her lack of understanding, not just of what was happening in her by virtue of her openness in that conversation but also of what Jesus meant by gifting the living water. At this point, this woman's patience and transparency have earned her another massive step in this process.

However, she stayed open. There was still one thing she had to do. She needed a humble descent as Jesus did at the start of the conversation. Jesus humbled himself by asking her for a drink. Likewise, she would have to do the same to collapse the boundaries between them so the living water could flow. But then she needed to be helped to attain this height of descent. Thus, Jesus makes another provocative statement, which may sound derogatory. Yet it is a necessary truth that must be told if this daughter of Samaria is to be brought to the truth that saves. He says, "Everyone who drinks of this water will be thirsty again, but those who drink of the water that I will give them will never be thirsty." The water that I will give will become in them a spring of water gushing up to eternal life." On hearing this truth, though a negative contrast to Jacob's Well, something happened to her. There was a thirst or longing for this other water that led to eternal life. This could have been Jesus pointing out to this daughter of Samaria what she had truly longed for but didn't know how to attain. "Sir, give me this water," she says, "so that I may never be thirsty or have to keep coming here to draw water."

At this, it seemed, the thing about the Jews and Samaria squabbles vanished, but not without openness, significant risk of offence, patience, and humility. When these are present, we would be surprised to see how many life-transforming encounters we would be having in most of our conversations.

Jesus could then dive into something more personal, having created a serene atmosphere of sincere desire, friendliness, and closeness. No one was standing at a lofty height at this point. "Go call your husband and come back," Jesus asked. "I have no husband," she replied. Jesus says, "You are right in saying, I have no husband, for you have had five husbands, and the one you have now is not your husband…." It was at this point that the woman recognized Jesus as a prophet. But little did she know that standing before her was One greater than a prophet - God Incarnate. On realising this, the Samaritan woman needed to understand where all this was leading to because something very crucial was still unresolved, something that would have been a concern for many Samaritans, and that was about the validity of the Samaritans' worship.

The question is really about the salvation of the Samaritans. Hence, she says, "Our ancestors worshipped on this mountain, but you say that the place where people must worship is in Jerusalem." This is a question that probably needed to be resolved since Samaritans were not allowed to worship in Jerusalem. She would have questioned in her heart, "How would your preaching to me be of any use because I don't necessarily want to become a Jew?" Jesus immediately acknowledged the truth but answered straight from the heart of the Father, who wants all people to be saved and not a particular sect. Jesus says, "Woman, believe me, the hour is coming when you will worship the Father neither on this mountain nor Jerusalem. You worship what you do not know. We worship what we know, for salvation is from the Jews. But the hour is coming, and it is now here when the true worshippers will worship the Father in spirit and truth. God is spirit, and those who worship Him must worship in spirit and in truth."

I can almost feel, as I write this, how these words would have been so soothing to this woman and the sense of peace and reassurance they would have brought her. Her gaze has now been turned from speaking and thirsting for Jacob's well (a symbol of the well of salvation) to speaking and thirsting for the living water and the coming Messiah (Christ). Jesus, seeing that she was now ready and in that place to receive the truth of who He was, said to her, "I am He (*ego eimi*) the one who is speaking to you." We are told she left her water jar and went back to the city to invite people to come and see Jesus. In Jn. 4:39, we are told many from that city believed in Jesus because of the woman's testimony, "He told me everything I have ever done."

If both (the Samaritan Woman and Jesus) had not walked the path of humble descent and openness, this encounter that led to the uncovering of wounds would not have happened.

Humility Opens the Door

God is still actively at work in our midst today. But more often than not, we shut him up. The human person is a conversational being. Humans realise their true self in the relationship with themselves, God, and their neighbours. This relationship is a journey fully realised in the attainment of the Truth. It then follows that our conversation, which is a major part of every relationship, must be protected. However, this protection should not entail always wanting it without any risk of offence. If our conversations with God and our neighbours would be anything real and life-giving, then openness to possible offence, patience, and humility must be returned to the table. Their absence makes people unable to engage in a truth-based conversation, hence incapable of authentically engaging in the noble but adventurous journey of pursuing the truth.

To breathe life into your conversations, let us think about those critical dispositions and practise them in real-time. We pray for the same grace the Samaritan woman had and operated with as Jesus gently led her through a life-changing journey.

Get Out of the Way and Allow Grace

Get out of the way and allow grace. This thought dropped into my heart on a Monday evening as I was on the London tube, heading back from chaplaincy work. It was too hot outside. As always, the underground was even hotter. I felt like standing since I had been sitting in meetings and performing other administrative tasks for a while. But then, I noticed, as I entered the tube, that a lady probably wanted to stand where I was. She had a suitcase with wheels that she dragged along. As soon as I saw her, I shifted to allow her to take my place and also have a spot to keep her suitcase. Surprisingly, she neither saw me nor noticed that I had moved away.

It was then that the words, "Chinedu, get out of the way and allow grace," dropped into my heart. Immediately, I brought out my phone and began to type away. I felt as if God was inviting me to step aside and let His grace work, so that He could fulfil His plans in my life. As I typed these words, I became a bit worried, thinking about ways I may have hindered the grace of God in my life. My heart went to various things. I wondered what I could be doing that I wasn't doing, or the things I was doing that had become a reflection of myself and not of God, even though they might appear very religious. One thing that was undoubtedly clear to me was that the word of God does not come to one in vain. God does not speak simply for the sake of speaking. When God speaks, there is always a purpose, a reason, and an invitation. And "as the rain falls and waters the crops and makes what is planted to grow, even so, is God's word" (Isaiah 55:10). However, God's word is not arbitrary, nor does it violate our will. Hence, by our will and choices, we can refuse to embrace the fulfilment of God's word in our lives.

But the question remains unanswered: how does one step out of the way of divine grace? Often, in our Christian journey of life, ignorance and pride can firmly stand in the way. However, this is where humility comes in. It helps the ignorant become aware of their ignorance and seek wisdom. For the proud, it brings one down from a false height that distorts one's vision and clears one's vision to see as God sees. Ultimately, the self is put in its proper place of grace, and God is allowed to be God, occupying the centre of one's life. Again, this is justice due to God.

Our Light in Darkness: Using Humility to Wait on the Lord

Fortunately, our faith does not always leave us on a mountaintop of certainty, hopefulness, clarity, and light. Sometimes, we experience what is often called the dark night of the soul when we feel as though we have lost our faith altogether. During this painful but fruitful process, if approached with the right attitude, we seem to lose the Christian's priceless gift of peace, joy, and the feeling of God's closeness. You could indeed say that one feels naked and exposed to darkness. You get a sense of this in many places in the scriptures. The psalmist would pray, "O Lord, you have taken away my friends, and my one companion is darkness."[33]

Although, at this time, the Christian might say many prayers and read as much of the Bible as possible, he/she increasingly finds him/herself dry and exposed. I could forget every experience I have had in my journey of faith, but never that of walking through this path that felt so lonely and scary. It was indeed a dark night. Strangely enough, my experience of this was mild compared to what I now see people experiencing. Yet, it was the most painful thing I have ever experienced, except for the death of my eldest brother Sergius, which took me years to grieve. When my brother died, my mind blocked it off. I knew pretty well that my brother had died because I was there when he was taken to the Morgue. I was also there when he was buried, but the pain was too much to bear then. Years later, just a few months before my diaconate ordination in London, I dealt with that through a gentle deliverance prayer called *Unbound* by Lozano.

My Experience

My experience of the dark night of the soul was scary but of a different type of emotion. It was my second year and my first semester at Allen Hall Seminary (Westminster Diocese). We had just returned to the seminary from summer vacation and were still unpacking and doing house meetings. The academic work hadn't started yet, so I was still arranging my room.

Right amid the excitement of meeting fellow seminarians, especially in the first years, I suddenly felt I had lost my faith. I could not understand what was happening. My Divine Office (the Church's official prayer) felt dry and meaningless. At some point, I wondered what I was doing in the Allen Hall Seminary. As a person who had always depended on the word of God, I felt a huge shock when the Bible became dry and felt like any other book. At first, I wasn't sure how to explain what was happening. I wished it was all a dream. Unfortunately, it was all real and happening to me. Holy Mass became a very tacky, detached, and meaningless show.

I must confess here that I really prayed all manner of prayers just to be able to breathe again spiritually. I felt like I was continuously sinking into this bottomless darkness. I would cry many times in my room and in the chapel, and I would usually get up in the middle of the night and go to the chapel to pray. As prayer increasingly became more difficult, since I didn't believe anymore, all I could do was cry, wipe my tears, and walk away. Such was the nakedness I felt. I constantly examined myself to see if something I did was so severe that God would decide to inflict me with such pain.

Seeking for Help

After a while, I decided to speak to a priest, but the challenge became who to pick, as what you don't want to do in such a state of vulnerability is fall into the hands of the wrong person. Providentially, my formator was an excellent and experienced priest, such that he obliged me as soon as I requested an audience with him. I remember walking into his living room that couldn't be distinguished from a library due to the number of books on the floor, table, side tables, and couch. I remember looking at all those books and thinking it was all a waste of time reading them. Having also given up on reading at this time, I equally envied him for being able to find interest in reading.

He immediately removed the books from the couch and asked me to make myself comfortable. Well, being comfortable was the least of my problems at the time. Perhaps, finding meaning and purpose was. After a moment of silence and pondering where to start, and literally in tears, I shared my ordeal with him. He listened intently while I went on and on, never interrupting me. As I shared my experience, I could feel from the other end a listening ear. When I finished, he said something along these lines, "Oh, Chinedu, I am sorry to hear that you are going through this." Then he shared his experience from many years before; I think he was a seminarian and about the same stage of formation as I was then. So, firstly, I felt understood and listened to.

He then gave me a few words of counsel. I don't exactly remember them word for word, but you would understand what I mean when I say it now. He said, "Chinedu, if you made a decision during a time of consolation, do not reverse it in a time of desolation. Hang on in there; it will pass." He then told me that he got that from Ignatian Spirituality. So, we chatted about how I was getting on with my studies and other things in the seminary. I thanked him and went to my room, repeating to myself, "In desolation, do not forget the times of consolation."

I repeated this line throughout the day, pondering what that meant, given my desperate situation. I was still lost, though. This sentence, which happened to be the only anchor I had, left me with so many questions: What does this mean? What do I do with this? How can this be helpful? I thought that my situation was probably a hopeless one if that was all my formator could offer me in that desperate moment, as I still felt lost.

However, after some weeks of going through this process, the repetition of those words began to change how I felt. At least, I thought it did. It could have simply been because the situation had lived its full course, the priest having also said, "...hang on, it will pass."

In His Time, God Makes All Things Right

But as I continued to repeat those words, I realised that I was beginning to relax a bit and was stopping the fighting to break through what felt like a strong wall around me. There was a sense in which I would say that I was beginning to embrace it as given by the Lord since the scripture says that, "The Lord gives death and life, brings down to Sheol and lifts up. The Lord makes poor and rich, he humbles and also exalts. He raises the poor from the dust and lifts the needy from the dunghill" (see 1 Samuel 2:6-8).

I remembered what Job 2:10 says: "If I received blessings from the Lord, shall I not also receive adversity from his hands." I must say that this realisation came very slowly, with time. It was becoming clear to me that what I felt I lost was a gift, which I sought, by all means, to get rid of, could as well be a gift from the Lord. Though I wasn't a hundred per cent convinced of this truth immediately, every day was an experience of learning to embrace my emptiness. And simultaneously, I was beginning to feel his presence again; perhaps, not so much in terms of feeling, but knowing that he was there regardless of how I felt.

Lessons For Me

In this recovery mode, I had time to reflect on what the words from the priest were asking of me and what they might actually mean. In my case, I realised that God was inviting me to consider the truth, that the feelings of desolation and consolation could both be God's gifts and, therefore, should be handled with care. I said 'in my case' because it may not be the same as another person's experience of the dark night of the soul.

I felt that God probably wanted to teach me that that which I treasured so much, e.g., my faith, was and will never be an entitlement. It is a free supernatural gift sustained by the giver, God. Even though it can often be challenging to accept, it then follows that it is not only the giving that is a gift; the taking could often, but surprisingly, be a greater gift. Often, in what we perceive as God's absence, we are invited to know God more profoundly or, rather, in a different way.

In my reflection, I realised that, through those words from the priest, the Lord invited me to humbly accept that both the faith I sought and the desolation I felt were all from Him, and that none had been as a result of any merit of mine; that only in humility would I eventually discover, amid this fiery experience, the

Fourth Man in the fire (Daniel 3:24-26). I realised that it would never be by throwing spiritual tantrums, as though what I had was the fruit of my hard work.

In retrospect, I realised that the more I struggled, the more I was forcefully sucked into a cloud of doubt and unbelief. However, the more I repeated those words and slowly abandoned myself to the Beloved, whose presence I could no longer perceive, the more I unconsciously floated on the water of grace. It is true that to lose what you have tasted in its sweetness can be very painful, e.g., faith. But the truth remains that I would have been without faith had He not given it to me in the first place. Though I had worked hard and diligently to fan my faith into flame, it was still by His grace that I believed.

So, as I walked that valley of darkness, it seemed I was invited to wait for the fulfilment of His promises, which do not deceive (Habakkuk 2:2-3). While my intention and desire to quickly overcome this dark night of the soul were sincere and holy, the invitation of the moment was not to overcome but to humbly submit in trust. Even when I did not know, perceive, or understand what God was doing, I was to humbly wait because all is by grace. In this way, humility is often the only option for the Christian and a beacon of light when all else appears to have failed. The Bible says: "Even though we walk through the valley of darkness, no evil would I fear, for thou art with me" (Ps 23). Should I walk through the waters, I will not sink beneath them. Should I walk through the fire, I shall not be consumed by it. For indeed, I know that you have redeemed me and that I am precious in your eyes (Isaiah 43). Therefore, I humble myself before the One, who alone can lift me.

...But not without the Risk of Offence

There seems to be a correlation between people's civilization and their sensitivity to each other's emotions. With people's 'civilisation,' words and actions become increasingly considered before they are undertaken or spoken. And this is very important if we are to coexist peacefully and respectfully. All this is in response to the divine attraction towards the ultimate good.

Whilst contemporary society may not always have the ultimate truth in mind in its governance, the tendency to naturally move towards its attainment is engraved in humanity's DNA. So, a society pursues a perceived truth through these sensitivities, politeness, careful consideration of words and actions in light of their effect on others. But then, in the pursuit of truth, we risk offending each other, not intentionally. In this way, offence becomes a necessary and sometimes possible risk of this exciting and serious adventure. It is serious because our salvation depends on knowing and acting according to the truth. "You shall know the truth, and the truth shall set you free" (John 8:32). So, like every serious adventure worth undertaking, there would be risks involved in pursuing a perceived truth. As we advance in civilisation, we increasingly master the art of eliminating most risks, but never all of them, as that would be unattainable.

We desire to eliminate all risks in life. But at the same time, wisdom is needed to acknowledge and accept the necessary risks that make life an adventure worth undertaking. For example, if two people passionate about opposing views came together on a TV show for a debate, ground rules would usually be established to ensure order. However, for this debate to be meaningful to the audience, who are also passionate about the theme in question, care must be taken to allow for the possibility of offence that could occur in the process. Sometimes, to prove their point and be authentic and truthful, they would risk offending the other. It may not be helpful to agree with someone who is thought to be making no sense. Instead, truth should be communicated and pursued with respect, wisdom, and right timing. This is a sign of maturity and authenticity, and the Holy Spirit gives us words when we don't have any.

There is, though, a sense in which the virtue of humility puts one in a similar situation. The Christian who truly seeks to practise the virtue of humility must necessarily accept and acknowledge the possibility of offence. By that I mean, people feeling aggrieved by your being true to yourself and your convictions. Drawing from the scandalous nature of the Cross, humility is beautiful but can be daunting, scandalous to onlookers, and could, in fact, be a cause of irritation. In the practice of humility, we are to necessarily accept the reality that we may be misunderstood and that our life may be very discomforting to many who may want us to be like them or be something we cannot or do not want to be. Humility declares the truth with a loud voice amidst the world of desperateness, pretence, and falsehood.

Humility Grounds One in the Truth

It is unrealistic to say that humility is the same as trying not to offend anybody and being peaceful. The reality is that sometimes the opposite is true. Humility grounds one in the truth. The truth, as we know it, can sometimes be very hurtful.

To be grounded in the truth, sometimes we must firmly and courageously walk against the raging tide of people's and even our emotions, sentiments, and expectations. Whilst we should never enjoy seeing people offended, humility might sometimes take you down the road of having to endure witnessing the pain of loved ones due to your adherence to the truth. Awareness of this truth is helpful if we must avoid being tricked and trapped in an endemic sentimental and emotional blackmail of the world, which has rendered many too immature, unreal, and ungrounded to engage with the realities of life.

Any theology or teaching that tries to present humility as a virtue void of these risks isn't true and cannot set one free. Humility, by its very nature, risks offence. To understand this truth, we must look at Jesus, who is the way, the truth, and the life. Then we would see that such was His experience and should be ours if we are to learn humility from Him. Therefore, humility is only lovable when we embrace the risks involved in the descent of humility.

CHAPTER 4

HUMILITY AND THE REVERSAL OF THE EFFECT OF THE FALL

What really was it about the Fall of our first parents, Adam and Eve? What was at the heart of the matter if not a question of trust? Could God be trusted? Adam and Eve were created in God's image and destined for the highest of lives, the eternal life of God Himself. Why did they 'fall' into the temptation to follow the path of the deceiver, a path of pride and covetousness (trying to take what is not rightly theirs), the very path that brought the deceiver down in the first place? For he (the devil) had thought in his heart, "I will ascend to heaven above the stars of God; I will set my throne on high; I will sit on the mount of assembly in the far north; I will ascend above the heights of the clouds; I will make myself like the Most High" (Is. 14:13-14).

Then the Bible adds, *"But you are brought down to Sheol to the depth of the pit...."*[34] Having failed and thrown down, he set out to bring humanity down from a height loftier than what he had lost. His strategy was to sell a false height as real, beautiful, and enticing. He presented this false height as what God was depriving Adam and Eve. To embrace this false height means to deny their true place and make God untrustworthy.

Without going into details of the account of the Fall, I wish to state here that, that singular decision of believing the deceiver and not God, as it were, spiritually launched the whole of humanity to a very lofty but false height, where we are stripped and left with fear, guilt, and confusion. Consequently, we lost touch with ourselves and meaning, as the place we coveted wasn't ours to take, nor could it ever be ours by human strength.

Hung on this false height, from where we can't ever come down by our strength, we were left without hope. Knowing fully well that only in truth can a human genuinely worship God (John 4), the deceiver rejoiced that he had snatched us away from the truth of ourselves, thinking we had lost everything. But God's unfailing mercy came for us in our darkest moment. God had to send his only Begotten Son, the Eternal Word, through whom all things were made (see John 1:1-14, 3:16), that he might restore in us what was lost, and fix and heal that which was wounded and strained. However, this would be a gradual process of reversal, of descent from this false height to our proper place, but this time with a clearer vision of who we are and a better glimpse of our glorious future.

This is why the Christian journey remains a journey of humility, continuous descent, a return to the truth of who we are and ought to be. It is a path and life of return to the truth, from that which is treasured by the world as a lofty height but to the Christian is simply a denial, a falsehood incongruous with our true humanity and purpose. To discern and examine our Christian growth, we should examine our lives through the truth-lens of humility.

Humility: A Weapon against the Vices of Jealousy and Envy

Our constant descent from this false height, as explained earlier, is one and the same as being conformed to Christ, growing in every way into Christ, and fully maturing with the fullness of Christ himself.[35] Aren't jealousy and envy, which the Christian must fight against with every strength and commitment, simply indicators of the Christian's need to descend from a lofty but false height? Perhaps I should zoom in closely on the effects of the false height from which Jesus' descent has freed and is constantly freeing us.

Naturally, when you take what isn't yours there is a sense in which you lack peace. Knowing it isn't your place brings an inherent fear and insecurity that could be constantly associated with the occupied place. What follows then is that this false height is maintained by other falsehoods or lies. Estranged from our true selves by the false elevation, we are unfortunately but simultaneously estranged from others as well. We lose the sense of unity among ourselves. As it were, unconsciously, we feel within ourselves this force that places "me" against "them," and vice versa. Others' blessings no longer appear as mine, and mine not as theirs. This continues in an endemic and potentially vicious circle.

This estrangement then leads to the problem of, why them and not me, and why me and not them? One is then launched into an overpowering tension of constantly trying to be above all others. This is exactly the devil's sin, trying to make himself like the Most High. So, jealousy and envy become wounds that can only be countered by the opposite of a false elevation of self:

- Humility
- A modest estimation of self
- A constant descent for the good of the other

True love can do this because its very nature presupposes

humility. Hence, love is not self-seeking and does not envy but rejoices in the truth.[36]

It is often the case that when the faithful struggle with envy or jealousy, it feels strange and painful to them. I know this from personal experience. One can almost feel the frustration as to why, being that one instinctively knows that these are incongruous with human nature, let alone the Christian nature. However, rarely do we make the connection between being envious or maliciously jealous and the lack of humility. Envy, which seeks and wishes to destroy the good in other people, is an indicator of an absence of love. But how can there be love when there is no humility? As Pope Francis says, "Without humility, love has no access."

So, if one is truly tired of envy and jealousy and would like to overcome these hydra-headed sins, then making the practice of humility one's constant quest is the way forward. Consider all the other things we have said about humility and try to practise them. As we grow in humility, a descent into the purifying fire of truth, we simultaneously increase and advance in love, which quenches the subtle but enslaving flames of envy and jealousy. While it could be said that these sins tempt all humanity, they are nonetheless fuelled by the fire of pride that often tells us that we deserve more than the rest. When that which I love is found in the hands of another, I am hurt that I was not the person in possession of it.

Humility: Burning Down the Walls of Division Among Us

Why these walls of division amongst us, even among those who claim to believe? Why are we often blind to our oneness? The

Christian who strives to be faithful to the command of oneness will always confront these and similar questions.

When we are truly in touch with the depth of our being, our oneness immediately becomes evident. But because we are not always in touch with this depth and are often stuffed with pride, all we see is our differences. At this latter level, we congregate against each other. Division occurs when there is a loss of being in touch with the depth of what it means to be human. And when we find division in the Church, the same is true. It may indicate a lack of touch with the depth of our life in Christ, the centre and force of unity. In his letter to the Christian community in Corinth, St Paul likens this to the immaturity of the infant and considers it unspiritual, saying:

"I treated you as sensual people, still infants in Christ. What I fed you with was milk, not solid food, for you were not ready for it, and indeed, you are still not ready for it since you are still unspiritual. Isn't that obvious from all the jealousy and wrangling that there is among you and from the way you go on behaving like ordinary people? What could be more unspiritual than your slogans, I am for Paul' and 'I am for Apollos'?"[37]

In the Church today, we see people lay proud claims to ideologies like liberalism, conservatism, ultra-conservatism. What exactly are those, if not signs of a lack of being in touch with the God who unites us? What makes us compulsively identify with these ideologies that divide us? When we lose touch with the foundation, we turn to ourselves, and realising the futility of turning to ourselves, we turn to other things and people for meaning and purpose. Put simply, when God is not the centre of one's life, we lose touch with the centre of unity and oneness. The result is division among us. Hence, St. Paul told God's people that neither Paul nor Apollos mattered, but God, who gives increase.

Consequent upon the fallen nature of humanity being raised in Christ, there are often many walls of division amongst us, both those we created ourselves and those created by others and various events of life. The Christian is called to navigate all those and, with diligence, preserve the unity of the Spirit through the bond of peace.[38] But this maze of division is complex, hence there are principal virtues needed to embark on this journey or process of spiritual maturation. No wonder St. Paul says, "With all humility and gentleness, with patience, bear with one another in love."[39] The walls of division among us require a strong force, the fire of all the Christian virtues, to bring them down. Humility, with its gentleness and patience, melts down these walls with its fierce heat of truth, without rupturing the chord of love.

Often, we see people who rightly condemn this divisiveness among us, especially in the Church. Unfortunately, however, they imagine that the best way to confront these divisions is to reach down from the lofty heights of authority, power, and holier-than-thou attitude, relying on one's understanding and experiences rather than from the lowly foundation of truth. When this happens, we miss out on the fact that descent into humility is the only tool that can bring us down from the false height where we have lost touch with the truth about ourselves, which reveals the foundational truth of our oneness in Christ.

Only in our constant touch with the new life in Jesus Christ, the centre of unity, the one in whose body the curtain of separation was torn and the walls of division broken, can we overcome the many walls of division amongst us, thus constantly growing into the full stature of Christ.[40]

Humility: A Decrease that Allows for Divine Increase

In his letter to the Ephesians (chapter 3), St. Paul prays that the Ephesian Christian community experience the fullness of God. For St. Paul, the principal means of attaining this state or privileged experience of being filled by God is through the experience of God's love. Hence, he prayed,

"That according to the riches of his glory, he may grant you to be strengthened with might through his Spirit in the inner man and that Christ may dwell in your hearts through faith; that you, being rooted and grounded in love, may have the power to comprehend with all the saints what is the breadth, length, height, and depth, and to know the love of Christ which surpasses knowledge, that you may be filled with all the fullness of God."

The context of this prayer was St. Paul's genuine and pastoral fear and concern that his numerous sufferings might discourage the Ephesians. Unknown to the Ephesians, St. Paul's strength did not come simply from his human strength but from God, precisely from his profound experience of God's love. This explains why he prays that they may draw strength from the same source of his strength, namely God's love. With the power of love, we can endure all things for those we have come to love so dearly and still be pleased that we were able to suffer for them. The scripture shows us this several times when the disciples were worthy to suffer for the Lord after his Resurrection, whom they had come to love so dearly. After the cruel treatment of St. Peter and other apostles, to stop them from preaching the Word of God, the Bible says that "the apostles left the Sanhedrin, rejoicing that they had been counted worthy of suffering disgrace for the Name."[41]

As we read the scriptures, what is not always immediately

apparent to most of us is how our love for God does not only aid our readiness to suffer for the beloved, but also to humble ourselves for the sake of love. Humility, in this sense, can result from love or the fruit of an experience of true love. When we truly love, we are not only willing to suffer for the beloved but also wish that they are better than us – like a true parent would pray that they may decrease so their child may increase. "He must increase, I must decrease."[42] This is a prayer and indeed the heart desire of the man Jesus acclaimed to be the greatest of all born of a woman.[43]

By the time we reach the third chapter of John's gospel, where John the Baptist confessed the truth and reality of the manifestation of the Messiah, and at the same time, the true desire of his heart, the people were beginning to think that John was the Messiah due to the way he witnessed to the truth and called God's people back to their true faith. Perhaps John the Baptist knew that some already believed he was the long-awaited Messiah. Hence, by confessing the truth of who Jesus is, he was able to direct the people to the truth of who the Messiah is. While this might sound very simple, it was a huge act of humility by John the Baptist. One full of self-importance would have taken advantage of that opportunity to pretend and usurp the position of the Messiah, since everyone would have probably believed him. He could have said to himself, "After all, I have really worked very hard to get to where I am, what stops me from appropriating this attention and fame whilst it lasts, at least until the rightful owner of the title surfaced."

Humility grounds us in the truth of who we really are, hence making us servants and lovers of the truth. "He must increase, and I must decrease." This confession of John the Baptist is, first and foremost, a reality of what must happen when we encounter the Lord when he comes: his light and presence begin to dispel our darkness and weaknesses. At the fullness of time, therefore, he becomes all in all. "And when all things have been subjected to Him, then the Son Himself will be made subject to Him who put all things under Him, so that God may be all in all."[44]

Secondly, this was also a confession of the true desire of a loving heart. Love leads to humility because true love wishes the other to be better and greater. Of course, this is not by any means a rejection of oneself but a longing for one's object of love. You want to be overwhelmed by what you desperately love. So, whilst we see in this confession the sacrificial dimension of John's faith, it is, in the end, a blessing for God to increase in us and for us to be filled by him, not by us. This desire of John the Baptist already looked forward to the perfection of love when we increasingly became one with God by allowing him to increase his life in us.

The Christian's call or destiny is such that, through experiential love, they gradually and constantly become more like God, being filled by Him. For having been created *ad imaginem Dei*, in the final analysis, God is to become all in all as we self-abase ourselves for our love and desire for Him. Hence, God must increase, and I must decrease.

Chapter 5

HUMILITY AND THE CHRISTIAN DISCERNMENT OF THE TRUTH

In Search of Truth

What is truth? This was Pilate's question to Jesus at his trial. It was a response to Jesus' claim that he was king. Besides, he also claimed that he was born for that same reason and had come into the world to testify to the truth. "Everyone who is on the side of the truth," he says, "listens to me." Here, he reveals the level of the world's ignorance before the pure light of truth. Jesus, the King of kings and Truth Incarnate, stands unrecognised by the worldly kingship, even with all the display of wisdom and might by the latter. The scripture reveals how Pilate became unsettled by this, going back and forth to see if he could avoid acting against whatever this Galilean claimed as truth. However, Pilate sought to understand what truth is, and through his question revealed the world's constant difficulty in perceiving truth.

One must, therefore, deliberately and consciously seek the truth. However, the truth is attained because God allows himself to be known through self-revelation. Thus, in the service of the truth, Christians must first acknowledge that left on their own they cannot attain the truth needed to navigate life both faithfully and fruitfully. With this understanding, those who approach should first acknowledge their limitations, which, contrary to causing them to cower before their weakness, now leads to openness. This openness becomes a worthy response to the noble cause and adventure of the pursuit of The Truth. In this way, the Christian takes on the servant attitude—a servant who is not wiser than the master. The Bible says, "Be not wise in your own understanding."

Christian Discernment

Christians who have yet to make discernment a constant feature of his/her life risks everything, and are bound to be overwhelmed by avoidable mistakes. An authentic Christian life is a life of discernment. In an online seminar titled *Discernment: A Christian Way of Life,* Prof. Gambino shared that, "Discernment is crucial for every good Christian."[45] For Gambino, discernment is not simply advised but crucial for anyone aspiring to be a good Christian.

I would say that discernment isn't just for Christians alone but for every human person. This is because the nature of human life is often shrouded in mystery and uncertainty that constantly invite us to take steps into the unknown.

So, what is discernment? Perhaps I should start with what discernment isn't and shouldn't be about. Discernment isn't focused on outcomes and goals but on God's will. The understanding it grants isn't for us to simply attain our set goals but to attain God's will. As the scripture says, "The children of Issachar had an understanding of the time; thus, they knew what they were supposed to do."[46] It is not about our timing but God's timing and purpose. Therefore, 'self' must not take centre stage if the process is to resemble anything like discernment. This means that, for one's own good, it is directed towards finding the meaning and purpose of one's life. To this effect, Pope Francis shared that, "Discernment has to do with the meaning of my life before the Father who knows and loves me, with the real purpose of my life, which nobody knows better than he."[47]

The reality, though, is that no one discerns in a vacuum. We always come with our baggage of experiences, culture, prejudices, and other weaknesses to that process of discernment, which first purifies in order to reveal.

Presuppositions of Christian Discernment

We know and see in part; therefore, we constantly need God's light for guidance. Discernment presupposes that the discerner acknowledges these limitations and believes that there is someone in whom all wisdom resides. And in the case of Christian discernment, these presuppositions shift one's attention from oneself to God. I would illustrate with a gospel account a classic example of Christian discernment.

The first chapter of the gospel of St. Luke is the account of the Annunciation. In that account, a divine messenger (the Angel Gabriel) suddenly appeared to Mary and hailed her, saying, "Hail Mary, the Lord is with you." Now, let's stop there and consider how significant this would have been. Clearly, this messenger would have been very strange to Mary, who was also terrified at this sight. The manner of this greeting unsurprisingly worried Mary, as she may have wondered about the meaning of the lofty greeting and the reason for addressing it to her.

Mary would have known that the Lord was with her because she was part of God's chosen people. But this emphasis on the Lord being with her as a person may have triggered more questions than answers. Still, she remained calm and acknowledged her lack of understanding. How do we know that she acknowledged her lack of understanding? By revealing Mary's thoughts to the readers, St. Luke tells us that, "Mary was deeply disturbed by these words and asked herself what this greeting could mean." However, this unsettled state of mind was necessary for what followed next, a radical journey away from one's plans and understanding, as it were, to the plan of another (God), whom the former (Mary) believed knew the way.

There was a sense in which the message the angel brought would upset an existing plan. Hence, the Evangelist carefully, but with great subtlety, shows the reader that Mary wasn't a purposeless woman who sat there awaiting a divine visitation. I know some would wish, and even suggest, that this was the case, but unfortunately, to assume this as a sign of respect for Mary would be doing just the opposite. Although Mary was expectant of the fulfilment of the ancient hope of Israel, she wouldn't have done that in idleness. Mary was busy with her life and dedication to God, but she still had earthly usefulness. We work as our God works. Hence, Jesus said, "My Father is always at work until now, and I am also at work" (Jn. 5:17). Perhaps, that was part of the reason for the specificity and urgency in introducing Mary in the account as a virgin betrothed to a man named Joseph.

Thus, the Angel Gabriel takes Mary deeper into the journey of discovery and total submission to God's plan and says, "Do not be afraid, Mary; you have won God's favour." These two statements are powerful invitations. Firstly, the invitation not to be afraid implicitly acknowledges Mary's worry and confusion resulting from the greeting. It would be ridiculous to see someone at peace and tell them to not be afraid. Such an invitation or encouragement is only used in times of fear or worry, whether justifiable or not.

The second invitation gives the reason for the first: "You have won God's favour." Knowing that we are favoured, blessed, chosen, and destined to glory, as St Paul describes in Eph. 1:1-14, serves as a helmet of salvation in times of fear and worry. Being favoured, therefore, Mary was not to be afraid of evil news (see Ps 112:7), for all things work together for good to those who love him, those he calls according to his purpose (see Romans 8:28).

Only after this did the Angel Gabriel announce the Good News, something unheard of, completely unprecedented, unnatural, and foolish for a human to dare imagine or assume its possibility. It is none other than the revelatory news that a creature (Mary) would conceive and bear her Creator, that the mortal would give birth to the immortal, and that humanity would conceive and bear its Saviour. "Listen, you are to conceive and bear a son, and you must name him Jesus. He will be great and called the Son of the Most High. The Lord God will give him the throne of his ancestor David. He will rule over the House of Jacob forever, and his reign will have no end." Even at this point, the core of this message hasn't been fully dropped yet. But Mary's curiosity is already mounting, for which she sought to understand how God's lofty and incredible plan was to be accomplished: "But how can this come about since I am a virgin?" With honesty and openness, Mary approaches the mystery. As it were, she wondered how her intention of remaining a virgin could be reconciled with God's will for her to conceive and bear the Son of the Most High.

Here, faith is the only way forward. What was required here was not a faith that claims to know it all, but a faith that is summoned to seek understanding. It seems that Mary is doing well with the fear and worry at this point. But then the question of how this can be arises. The brilliancy of God's descent begins to blind the human senses and calls them to rise on the wings of faith to grasp the mystery. It was as if the Divine Descent needed human descent for the Incarnation to occur.

So far, this process has been challenging. But there was a constant and dynamic process of descent, first from God, whose descent always anticipates our descent. It is principally about God's will, not Mary's. It is about God's plan concerning Mary. So, in the end, it was for Mary's and the rest of humanity's good, but not with Mary at the centre of things.

Mary had already made massive progress from being afraid and disturbed to being curious and seeking understanding. However, she allowed herself to be led into that mystery, and she had clearly shown that she had no clue what that meant. Now the angel Gabriel will redirect Mary's focus from herself so she can understand how this impossible event would be possible. As long as Mary considered the possibility of the impossible in the light of what she could or could not do or offer, she wasn't going to access the realm of impossibilities.

Consequently, the Angel responds to her honest question about how and says, "The Holy Spirit will come upon you, and the power of the Most High will cover you with its shadow." See the high point of the encounter: the Angel continues, "And so the child will be holy and will be called the Son of God." The use of this title, "Son of God," after the explanation of the how, takes on a different dimension and clarity. Now Mary sees that this conception will only be brought about through the action of the

Holy Spirit in her, without any man. This later use of "Son of God" in Luke 1:35 clarifies the initial use of "Son of the Most High" in Luke 1:32. Mary would have understood clearly that the child she was to conceive was God. Even though this would have caused overwhelming joy in Mary, she nonetheless would have felt a great shock, heaviness, and a sense of unworthiness at the same time. But knowing that the Holy Spirit would bring this about, however, introduced a fresh air of relief into this short but intense encounter.

To fan Mary's faith into flame, the angel testified of her kinswoman Elizabeth's pregnancy. She was brought to see how the one whom everyone called barren has now conceived and is in her sixth month. Therefore, Mary's belief might be strengthened not to doubt what the Angel had said in Luke 1:37, "For nothing is impossible to God." And this is the point to which God has always wanted to lead Mary, a state where she overcomes fear, humbly acknowledges and accepts her limitations, relies not on her understanding but seeks understanding with faith and humility, shifting the focus from herself and her capability to God's.

Finally, she would say the great YES, FIAT, "Let what you have said be done to me." This is an ascent of faith which couldn't have been possible had Mary not experienced the descent of humility.

The Descent and Ascent of Humility in Discernment

In this account, a noticeable double-layered, simultaneous movement moves at parallels without contradiction in their internal work.

At one level is the descent, which is Mary's process of

recognising her limitedness, both in knowing and doing. In knowing, we can almost see the divine wisdom shining so brightly and revealing Mary's limited knowledge. For Mary, the way to deal with this huge gap between her understanding and the content of the Annunciation was not to deny but to **acknowledge and embrace it**, and, consequently, embrace our humanity. In revealing her limitedness, God revealed her greatness, because despite her limited knowledge, she embraced the truth and yielded to divine wisdom.

In doing so, Mary, having acknowledged her limitedness in knowing, also acknowledged that the content of the Annunciation's good news wasn't possible by her human strength. Nor could it ever be brought about by any human. However, she wasn't being dismissive, as we often are when we don't understand and fail to see the possibility of what the gospel presents us. She was open. She was willing to contribute to the accomplishment of this divine plan. Her openness and trust then made up for her lack of knowledge on how this event would come about in the one who speaks. This is to whom she now makes herself vulnerable by acknowledging her state before the overpowering mystery of the Incarnation.

Simultaneously, this *descent* is met in her by an *ascent* of faith. Certainly, her descent is indeed the Christian ascent, since our way up is down, and vice versa. As she descends in humility, she simultaneously ascends in faith to the possibility of the impossible.

One may argue that this biblical account does not accurately represent the typical discernment experience of most Christians. That is true. However, whether it is a short- or long-lasting discernment, the process and, indeed, the divine invitation and response could be said to be similar. Surely, most of us wouldn't be privileged enough to have an angel speak to us as clearly as Mary did. But the internal character of any discernment of God's will and plan is similar. It is dynamic and involves the Christian as much as it involves God. There is a journey to be made and we don't lead the way. God helps us in our weakness because he knows us better than we know ourselves. He acknowledges our fears and worries and reassures us of his fatherly care and protection. This trust is necessary for healthy discernment, mainly as the Lord takes us through what I call the 'maze of unknowing' that comes as our natural senses begin to fail us. This is so that we can turn away from ourselves to the Other, namely, God.

Within this journey, another essential part is acknowledging the truth about our limitedness in 'knowing and doing,' as I will explain later. Hence, we humbly seek understanding from the Other, namely, God. Gradually, and by grace, we learn to turn away from ourselves as the centre of focus and towards God, whose will and plan for our lives is the focus. If we are patient, as Mary was amid all the incredible things the angel said, the Holy Spirit will shine light upon our perceived impossible situations. Then we would see, as God sees, that the impossible can be possible by God's divine power, even if we don't know the how. I call this a penetration into the realm of miracles, where the impossible is made possible. When the angel Gabriel explained how and by whom this impossible would happen, Mary did not understand in detail. However, she then knew by whom it was to be accomplished.

Therefore, discernment does not imply knowing in full. In our Christian discernment, the aim isn't to know the full details, which is a gap that our faith fills, but rather to know God's plan and expectations. Even then, this is not fully known except in the measure His grace offers, which is just enough for each step of faith. Discernment could take time and leave us confused. However, in the process, we are changed so that we may be able to recognise and say yes to His will when it is revealed. This now requires the descent of humility, which is presupposed by the art of discernment.

Therefore, before attempting to start serious discernment, I recommend you pray for humility. Even after you have begun the discernment process, continue to ask God for the grace of humility. Be conscious of when the Spirit pulls you towards a descent of humility. It is in this descent of humility that we truly experience the true ascent of faith, which is needed to hear and see God, and thus stand in His will.

CHAPTER 6

HUMILITY AND OUR ORIGINALITY

The Pressure of Authenticity Today

There will continue to be increasing pressure and effort to remove, or at least diminish, every individual's distinctiveness in our world. Whilst this movement often hides under the guise of freedom and equality, it is nonetheless a dangerous trend. Moreover, there is a sense in which it dehumanises the human person, whose end can only be attained if one is true to oneself, thus preserving one's originality. In an attempt to defend our rights or those of others, care must be taken to not try to make everyone the same. Nor should we try to become another person. Everyone occupies a particular and distinctive place in the created order, a role no one else can play. This is the very reason why the death of any one of us permanently changes the created order. Likewise, each individual's inherent distinctiveness in the internal workings of the created order is completely special.

However, with the increasing pressure from the so-called pluralist and group identity propaganda, an enormous amount of pressure is mounted on individuals to the point of exterminating their distinctiveness and originality. The question then becomes: How can you consistently be yourself if you constantly try to become someone else, invented by some ideologue? The immediate consequence is the increasing loss of internal joy and fulfilment, hence distorting the created order.

The problem with this mode of thinking arises when we confront our weaknesses. Sometimes, with the invasive voices of social media, we are tormented by dangerous ideas of who we should be, how we should act, how we should look. Thus, we are unconsciously conditioned to think in a particular way, a mode of thinking we can't say is ours. Nonetheless, it impels us, subtly and, in some cases, forcefully, to become someone else, an image portrayed presented to me as the ideal. All these gradually blur the vision of my originality and the privileged place I occupy simply by the grace of my creation and existence, a place in which alone I am the best. This is what is meant by the expression, "Be the best version of yourself."

This war against the originality of the individual person cannot be overcome with only motivational writings and speeches. While these are helpful, they are simply not enough. Humility, however, is the antidote, the weapon against such invasive distortions in the knowledge of ourselves that has left so many dissatisfied and unfulfilled. But the question is, how can I consistently argue that I should remain myself when all I see when I consider my weaknesses or look into the mirror is the opposite of what I would like to be? It could be one's physique, or accidents like nationality, background, family, class, gender, colour. Oftentimes, these are things we don't have control over. For others, it could be things like their faith and beliefs, accent, IQ, likes and hobbies. Whilst we can always do our best to improve ourselves in order to be the best we can be, this improvement must be congruous with one's originality, that privileged role that, by the grace of creation and existence, you alone do occupy. Being made in the image and likeness of God, we know God does not make mistakes.

Unfortunately, the tendency is often to deny whatever we perceive as negative in us, which then leads to the denial of who one is and a constant but exhausting quest to be another. Thanks to God for his free grace of humility that aids our acceptance of ourselves, not in comparison to anyone, but in the light of who we are created to be, in the light of God's purpose and will. We often want to be another person due to a lack of knowledge of ourselves and the Other (God). That other person's image then becomes the object of our admiration.

You could argue that you truly know yourself, but there is usually something missing, which is where the beauty of humility shines out more brightly and powerfully. As I have tried to explain earlier, humility would mean knowing who we are before God and our neighbour. Then, for the sake of charity, we should refuse to cling to that which we have come to know but, through self-abasement, "give it back." In other words, you are constantly having to rely on God's vision and will to inform your knowledge of yourself. This is indeed a gift.

Taking this to be what humility means, in confronting our frailties and all the undesired areas of our lives that might be the truth and our living reality at the time, we must not cling to them. We give them back to God. The truth is that, from a false height of pride, looking down on ourselves, we are never good enough. This is because from a false height, that unlawfully elevated height, our visions are distorted, including our vision of ourselves. Our weaknesses or family background, skills, sex, and the like, are not the problem here. The problem is where we stand and view from. A humble heart sees through the lens of God. Obviously, it is not exactly like God, who is humility personified, but something very close to his vision.

Having seen their failures and weaknesses, those who are humble know that God's vision of their eternal destiny and beauty by far outweighs the former. Hence, the humble are not as disgusted by themselves as the proud. In clinging to the unmerited favour, the Christian confesses that the righteousness possessed in Jesus and the life now lived is not of them but of Christ who lives in them. Even then, the soul sees its uniqueness more clearly despite its sins and frailties. I dare say here that all persons are unique in every way, including their righteousness and sin. Only with the eyes of humble faith can one accept the hard truth that if we only strive to become others, it will only end in failure.

Humility brings one home to oneself and your uniqueness. It shields one from unhealthy and pride-driven escapism from oneself, which insists on the idea that I can't accept who I really am. I have to escape from being myself to becoming these 'ideal' images staring at, and even harassing me. I am going to risk everything to become that person. I do not care about what it means beyond the surface to be that person. Thus, a lack of humility sets one on the path of running away from the only place one can call and be at home, while risking everything to do that. In this situation, one is lured out of safety by the strange, false beauty of the lofty height of pride.

Only in oneself is the human person safe, and they can abundantly bear lasting fruits. You might not be the best by the world's standards, but you are that which another can never be, and so are the best in that way. You may have many weaknesses and flaws, yet you are the delight of God. You may have failed and would still fail many times, but you are not a failure. With the right attitude and humility, which help one stick to one's originality, your best will come in time. In being your best, there is no competition. Embrace the ground truth of humility, and make it difficult for such negative emotions as anxiety, jealousy, envy, low self-esteem, to overwhelm you. Your strengths and weaknesses combine to make you the best version of yourself. Therefore, I dare you to be your original self; do not be a pushover. Refuse to be lured by the false 'ideal' images of our time as the images to which you are to conform. It certainly will not be easy. There are many difficulties and challenges along the way, especially in our time and age. However, anything outside the humility path ends up in emptiness, an unfulfilled life, and unhappiness.

Do Yourself a Favour and Be Humble

The misconception of humility as a virtue that limits a person contributes to a more dangerous misunderstanding of the virtue. Consequently, humility has come to be seen as self-deprivation. Humbleness is often misconstrued as being only directed to the other and their good, with nothing in stock for the humble. In this sense, it appears as self-neglect and privation. Perhaps, it would be important to consider this thinking process that makes humility a victim of suspicion.

The account of the Fall shows us how humankind's attempt to be at the centre of all things led to humanity's catastrophic loss, confusion, and shame. Why such a desperate attempt to be at the centre of all things? It all comes down to suspicion and a lack of trust. But these did not, nor could they have originated from humankind. Unfortunately, having been deceived by Satan in Eden to desire to be at the epicentre, thereby becoming the measurement of all things, man and woman realised to their rude shock that they could never attain such a position, being incompatible with their nature.

In this disobedience, humanity found itself in a place where it needed to descend by accepting its state as a creature dependent on God; not in control, not the measure of all things.

Instead, we constantly seek to be at the epicentre, getting upset and unsettled by anything that reminds us of the truth of who we were created to be. Hence, humility becomes unnatural to us because it moves us away from our false self-perception as the centre of all things. The problem is this: we can't trust another to be the centre and measure of everything. It first has to be about us. To put it bluntly, we struggle to accept we were created to be human and can never realise the false images we portray. Hence, peace and happiness elude us, resulting in confusion. Humility is, therefore, a favour we must each do to ourselves.

Contemporary society isn't yet free from this age-long pattern of thinking, that we should be at the centre and the measure of everything. Isn't that why we rupture our relationship with the created order, treating it as if we are the end of all things, and forgetting that the Great Injunction of Genesis 1:28 is about stewardship, not dominance? Of course, our quest for dominance equally extends to how we use our bodies. Yes, our bodies belong to us, but our use of it must be consistent with the purpose and meaning of our creation. Indeed, when humility is lost, all things lose their divinely assigned place in the created order.

There is an apparent forgetfulness of the truth that humility could not have been useful to anybody had it not been suitable to the moral subject himself. If humility, as some claim, helps others at all, then it would be because it had borne good fruit in the humble. In humility, one finds their true self and the foundational purpose of life.

If humility places one in good relationship with oneself, the created order, one's neighbours, and with God, then it cannot be that it only benefits the other to whom it is directed. This healthy relationship bears fruits first for the humble, who is now rightly placed to engage fruitfully with the world, knowing their true place in the scheme of things; their vision of themself and others is healthy. Thus, standing on the truth of who and whose they are, they engage rightly and fruitfully with other things and are consequently happier. So, the humble is the first reaper of the fruits of the invaluable virtue of humility. The Christian only does himself a favour by being humble.

When the purpose and meaning of humility is lost, it is misconstrued as weakness, ignorance, timidity, low self-esteem, self-neglect, and often the humble is viewed in the light of one, more, or all of the above. But beyond these negative views of humility, there is a subtle but dangerous notion that humility is simply for others and has very little to offer the moral subject.

Spiritual Lightness

To experience what I have called 'spiritual lightness,' the Christian is to allow for the shedding of the weight of pride. In John 14:6, Jesus says that "He is the Way, the Truth, and the Life. But he also said that he is the gate."[48] Elsewhere, he talked about the Way that leads to life as a narrow path, and due to its narrowness, few people are found there (Matt 7:14). He nonetheless makes it clear that this road is navigable. Hence, he says, "Strive to enter, because many will try but will not enter" (Luke 13:24). The questions to ask, though, are: In what way is this Way narrow? What makes it narrow so that only a few walk therein?

Whilst every path in life comes with its challenges, as none is easy, the narrowness of the Christian way is associated with the weight or heaviness of the baggage of pride and other vices in the human heart. The problem isn't with the road and its narrowness, which has existed since the beginning, as much as we were created to travel that path delightfully. If we struggle (which we all often do) to walk the way, the problem is with us and what we have become. Therefore, we must return to who we truly are: frail creatures, dependent on God, without whom we can do nothing. This act of returning to the truth of who we are is indeed humility. Thus, I said that humility grounds us in the truth.

There is a sense in which Jesus' words in Matthew 7:14 and Luke 13:14 suggest that to walk in this Way, which is the truth, the Christian must be ready to enter that spiritual process of shedding the weight of pride. Pride heavily burdens the Christian's spirit and makes it take paths unaided by grace. It makes one take on a way or mode of living that is unsustainable, even by the grace of truth. One's yoke becomes heavier with this likely unintentional denial of grace and truth through falsehood. Consequently, this makes our Spirit unable to mount and fly on the wings of humility that should help us take on Jesus' lighter yoke. To be spiritually light, we are to heed Jesus' words in Matthew 11:29-39, "Take my yoke upon you and learn from me;

for I am gentle and lowly (humble) in heart, and you will find rest for your souls. For my yoke is easy, and my burden is light." In the final analysis, humility is first and foremost for the good of the humble, whose yoke is made lighter.

Humility, Truth, and Oneness with Oneself

In my few years as a Catholic priest, and in the light of the many conversations I have had with God's people, I have come to appreciate more the importance of humility in living an authentic Christ life. "Learn from me; for I am gentle and humble in heart" (Matthew 11:29). When carefully contemplated, Jesus seems to be saying in this verse that the reason for discipleship is because of his gentleness and humility. Whilst gentleness or meekness could be seen as being able to keep strength under measured control, humility is the context which gives it purpose and direction and culminates into being one with oneself whilst taking other virtues and fruits of the spirit into view.

Having assented to faith, the Christian is called to go beyond the mere confession of faith in words to believing in their heart and finally practising the confessed and believed truth. Often, the Christian, striving to conform more closely to Christ, is caught in a tension between these three, as there is often a vast or subtle disparity among them. The priest, as he goes up to the altar to say Mass, would ask God for unity amongst these three in these similar words, "...that what I say with my lips, I may believe in my heart, and what I believe in my heart, I may practise and show forth in my daily life." This acknowledges that the Christian upward calling is directed towards attaining this unity or oneness. Therefore, it can be argued that true Christian joy is in some way relative to how this tension is lived truthfully.

The narrower the gap between these three stages, as it were, the greater the experience of Christian joy and peace. The wider the gap, the more the Christian experiences the lack of true peace. This is an existential human reality, as it were, grafted into our DNA right from our creation. God is one in Himself, His word, and His actions. We are created in God's image (*ad imaginem Dei*, as St. Augustine argued) so that with our free will, intellect, and the help of the divine grace, Christians may become one with themselves, thus becoming the beacon of unity and truth in the world. From this oneness then flows our common Christian unity, which Christ prayed for. But if the Christian isn't making conscious effort to live this tension healthily, neither can they be able to maintain the bond of unity with other Christians, as they will be torn apart within. As the scripture says, "No bad tree bears good fruit…The good man brings good things out of the good treasure of his heart, and the evil man brings evil things out of the evil treasure of his heart."[49] The Christian cannot offer the oneness that Jesus earnestly prayed for in John 17 if they hadn't first begun to experience interior oneness or unity.

The truth is, that Christians often find themselves in tension as they perceive the disparity between what is confessed, believed, and lived out. Thus, the Christian's journey consists of continuously and carefully acknowledging this tension. It requires an astute discernment of the inner workings of the Holy Spirit, with whom, through our openness, we strive to reduce this disparity. This is through our close conformity to Jesus, in whom we live this reality with a living hope. With humility, the Christian acknowledges the reality of this constant tension but decides to confront it with the help of grace. This is a constant reality as long as we are in the earthen vessel, which is our body, with all its weaknesses; humility helps to reconcile this painful but healthy conflict in us.

As St. Paul wrote to the Christian community in Rome, talking to them about the salvation that God offered to all people (Jews and Gentiles through grace (Rm. 5:1) and the hope (Rm. 5:5) that came through Jesus Christ. He also talked about his experience of this Christian struggle. In the seventh chapter of his letter to the Romans, St. Paul says, "What I want to do, I do not do. What I hate I do…for in my inner being I delight in God's law." Important to note here is that St. Paul seems to suggest that this is a common struggle as a believer. Having brought this reality of the Christian to the surface, which leaves them helpless and without hope of ever succeeding, St Paul then offered a humble acceptance of what has been offered in Christ as the faithful remedy. Thus, he added, "Thanks be to God, through Jesus Christ our Lord!"[50] What St. Paul finally did was accept the truth humbly, the reality of his situation. However, in hope, he humbly submitted to the grace offered by Christ Jesus.

In the humble acceptance of this truth of our struggle and the openness to the help of the Other (God), this endemic, eternal struggle could ever be reconciled.

Humility and the True Love of Oneself

Lack of love or hatred for oneself often finds its root in pride, which makes it impossible to accept one's state, a state that often falls short of one's expectations.

True love is truth, and grounds the lover and the beloved in the truth. Thus, we cannot truly love from a place of falsehood. When we talk about the lack of love in our world or the difficulty of living a life of true love in our time, we are actually talking about the problem of falsehood coming from a lack of humility. This is because, from an elevated height of falsehood, the truth of love becomes challenging to give or receive.

But how can a self-hating person possibly love others? That's impossible, since love firstly presupposes an acceptance of oneself with all its weaknesses, shortcomings, and inadequacies, and as one capable and worthy of loving others. Only then can one venture into accepting and excusing other people's inadequacies and loving them regardless. However, this self-acceptance requires the humility with which to accept our weaknesses and realities under the light of faith and the power of grace, which manifest in weaknesses (see 2 Corinthians 12:9).

True love presupposes humility. Pride numbs the heart and hardens it from experiencing the moisture and softness necessary for the seed of love to thrive. Therefore, the one who struggles with loving oneself should pray for and practice humility. That means that we all need to pray, then.

Chapter 7

HUMILITY AND INSECURITY

Insecurity as a Universal Experience

Human insecurity is a reality experienced by every person at varied times and degrees. As it were, it comes in different forms and bears different fruits in different people. It is, therefore, a psychological state of vulnerability that arises from a perceived limitation of one's strength or capability against a perceived danger, situation, challenge. These elements or situations strip away a previously perceived shield, security, or protection, or at least render it not as efficacious as one might have thought.

It may be correct to say that every person might have or will experience this at some point in life. Whilst this may be wholly private and appear utterly unnoticeable to others, it is a common human reality that can be good. For some, a sudden feeling of insecurity has made them discover an unknown aspect of their lives. For others, it has become a reclining step to the foundational base of humility. For the spiritually minded, it could lead to reaching out to others and God for help.

However, a feeling of insecurity could exacerbate and spread like a hydra-headed pandemic, to the point of crippling an individual. It was not until I became a chaplain to a charity organisation for the homeless in London that I witnessed how crippling the feeling of insecurity can be. Usually, I would offer spiritual and religious support to our clients who were mostly homeless, some with post-traumatic stress disorder (PTSD), and others with substance misuse problems. I must say that some of the insecurities I have witnessed in our clients were mostly due to their previous challenging experiences. Hence, they were not able to move past the post-traumatic effects. But often, I have met some who, for other reasons, including mental health challenges, had become so paralysed that they couldn't do anything for themselves, let alone others.

For the few years I worked there as a chaplain, I realised the clients who did well were those who walked the path of humility, which is the path of truth, as opposed to the path of falsehood. They were clients who, with the support of our staff, accepted the truth about their situation and actually did or tried to do what was necessary to transform their lives. Often, they had to arrive gently at a point where they would start stripping away every false protective, shell-like façade before they could ever feel the effect of the transformative change of the services offered to them.

As everyone would do, when they first present themselves at the service, there is that insecurity, mainly because they don't know what to expect. Sometimes, they think they will be judged, for which they erect a wall of resistance against our approach. Whilst some would present untrue stories, others would withhold details, often forgetting the part they would have to play in our effort to support them. For instance, and funnily so, a client could come in and claim to not intend to bother anybody nor depend on the system. While this could be how they truly felt, in the final analysis, what matters is their actual need, which requires that they 'bother' us, the staff. Understandably, the statement, "I do not want to bother anyone," is simply a wish. But reality is often different from wishful thinking, which is usually denial in disguise.

Furthermore, we find people who, through falseness or sheer human weakness, pass through the system. For them, it is a way of ascent, whilst, in reality, it is a descent, as lies can only offer a false, feeble foundation. Yet, some people are open and sincere. Between both sets of clients, the latter has, in my experience, shown to have had a more lasting transformation.

I find in the approach of the latter set of clients a profound humility. Humility is truth, which alone can carry and surmount our crippling insecurities that are often justifiable but, in the end, find their source in our wounded nature. A solid foundation of humility is needed to overcome, or at least learn to deal with, most of our insecurities. While living from a false height is a constant invitation for fear and insecurity, to be grounded in humility is to have a firm grip on the truth, which sets us free. This would require a prayerful, deliberate, and constant striving to walk the humble, narrow path that leads to true joy and peace.

Humility: A Tilled Soil for Authentic Christian Living

As a boy, I remember going to the farm with my parents, though mainly with my dad. Both my parents were civil servants; teachers, precisely. However, they supported their earnings with farming by cultivating some of our food. Initially, I was fascinated by farming. I craved it, asking, even as a child, to be allowed to go with my parents whenever they did. However, when I finally came of age to do proper farm work, it didn't take long before I realised it wasn't fun. Indeed, it was tedious work.

Neither rain nor sun stopped us from farming. During a new farming season, the ground would usually be cleared, tilled, and, in most cases, made into ridges and mounds. We planted all manner of crops at a subsistence level, only for household consumption. But among the many things that fascinated me about farming was how important it was for the soil to be tilled and softened for the crops to germinate. And even after a seed has navigated through the soil and come to the surface, during weeding, the soil is further softened and with more support provided the base of the crops.

Water was obviously essential. However, without the tilling and softening of the soil, the crops struggled and, in most cases, died. Therefore, the tilling and softening of the soil aided the penetration of water, the easy sprouting of the seeds from the ground, and the deepening of the roots into the ground. To add manure to the soil, we still needed the soil to be tilled for a good mixture of the manure.

I intend to use this analogy to illustrate the place of humility in our Christian faith. Humility is like the tilled soil of the Christian life, within which other seeds of the Christian faith grow or are aided to grow. The water, manure, etc., are like the other graces or virtues in our lives, which, as it were, would experience a kind of stunted growth or, in a more serious case, be stifled to death should the soil not be tilled. The tilling of the soil symbolises the act of humility, the conscious and purposeful self-abasement, which then provides a tilled soil (a conducive atmosphere) where the seeds of faith could grow.

Furthermore, the tilled soil of humility makes it easier for unwanted seeds and plants to be uprooted from our hearts and lives, a typically painful experience. A heart tilled by humility feels less pain because it is easier to uproot from moistened soil than from dry soil. Likewise, a heart tilled by humility leads to fruitfulness as it aids spiritual fertility.

The gospels point to this truth in the parable of the sower in Mark 4:8 and describe this soil as good soil, which brought forth grain, growing up and increasing and yielding thirtyfold and sixtyfold, and a hundredfold. This parable immediately asks the question: How is the soil of our hearts tilled so that the seed of God's word from the sower might find in us fertile soil? Our immediate reaction would be, "Hold on!" God's word is supposed to help till and prepare the hearts, as we see in St. Luke's post-Resurrection experience of Cleopas and companions in Luke 24:13-35.

God's Word Tills the Soil of our Hearts

In that account, we see how, in the breaking (explaining) of the word (scriptures), the downcast hearts of Cleopas and his companion were set on fire and prepared to encounter the Risen Lord at the Breaking of Bread (Eucharist). So, their unprepared hearts were prepared by God's Word. In this case, the seed of God's Word carried within it the grace that simultaneously prepared and tilled the hearts with its coming.

On the contrary, if I may, there is a sense in which the parable of the sower presupposes an already prepared heart that is now met with the seed of the gospel. How can a heart be prepared without God's word, merits, and effects? Is the scripture simply leaving the moral duty of preparing the heart to the moral subject (the person themselves/the reader)? Well, the hard truth is yes and no.

First, let us look at the 'no.' God is not abandoning the frail moral subject in preparing the heart for the seed of God's word to bear fruit. God's word carries within it a grace that completes our often tiny preparedness. Besides, it is the Lord who gives the power to will and to do (Philippians 2:13) for his good pleasure. "It is not of him that wills or runs, but of the Lord that shows mercy" (Romans 9:16). In the end, we are not alone, in so far as the sacred freedom of the human agent remains inviolate by the Divine Agent.

Yes, by free will, the Lord allows us to do our bit. This is a necessary Divine Act of love if the human agent must not become passive in their salvation, or God would become so involved in such a way that it loses integrity. Since the Christian is, to a great extent, an active participant in this process of their salvation, the word of God is gentle and cannot force itself onto a heart, nor would it do for one that which is within one's duty and limit to do by grace. Even with divine grace, the individual (the moral subject) is constantly invited to openness and acceptance of what is offered. And through this constant acceptance and docility to God's will and plan, a heart comes into that process of readying or preparing itself for the sowing of the seed of salvation. So, openness is needed even when a person is perplexed by the events in their life.

Hence, in the twentieth verse of the parable of the sower (Mark 4:8), Jesus elaborates on verse eight, which I referred to above, and says, "But those that were sown upon the good soil are the ones who hear the word and accept it and bear fruit, thirtyfold, sixtyfold, and hundredfold." As used here, the word "accept" would mean much more than just saying yes to God's word. It entails a concrete commitment to and living out God's word, which often takes us to places of discomfort and, in some cases, embarrassment.

Faithfully accepting and living God's word doesn't always make us look wise or famous in the sight of the world. The opposite is often the case.

Humility and courage, therefore, become the way of life, God's Way, as Pope Benedict XVI said. It then follows that the Christian life, which consists in knowing and following Jesus (Jn 10:27-31), the Way, the Truth, and the Life (John 14:16), would be impossible without the Humble Path, the path of the cross (Philippians 2). Without humility, the word of God is often not accepted for what it is, God's word, not some human thinking (1 Thessalonians 2:13), or easily dismissed as irrelevant. A heart untilled, or rather not being tilled, by humility rejects and questions God's word and cannot do otherwise. Thus, even with the best of intentions, the heart would still be closed to it.

As it pertains to the tilling of human hearts for fruitfulness, the virtue of humility becomes very decisive and critical. Let us be deliberate and conscious in our practice of true Christian humility and see how our hearts would and could, like the soil, be tilled, ready, and receptive for fruitfulness.

CHAPTER 8

HUMILITY AND BEING AFLAME WITH GOD'S LOVE

Before I joined the Catholic Charismatic Renewal in 1999 in southeast Nigeria, I was always fascinated by the lives of its members. The enthusiasm, passion, and zeal with which they worshipped God and evangelised in word and deed had me attracted to the movement. Whilst many had joined due to the movement's conversion of souls outreaches, most remained members because of the fraternal love and sacrifice they experienced therein. The most moving experience I had in this group was the joy they radiated and, certainly, the love shown to me – our philosophy of life being, "To be aflame with God's love."

I didn't quite make much of the life until later in life when I had the opportunity to reflect on what was happening back then. Obviously, in hindsight, I could see some of our 'innocent' mistakes. No doubt, we could have done things better. But again, isn't that what life is about? We live and learn, and most often through our mistakes, especially when the people who were supposed to teach and instruct us distance themselves, preferring to criticise from afar.

Reflecting on the expression, "To be aflame with God's Love," and placing it side-by-side the life we lived over those years and, of course, with the experiences of God's power that accompanied it, I have come to identify its connection with the life of humility among the members. By the way, this is by no means an attempt to say there weren't members who had pride issues. Certainly, there were. Perhaps, I was among those who, like an uncut diamond, needed to discover the path of humility, an ongoing purifying process of descent.

However, I would say that the practice of humility and being aflame with God's love reinforce each other. The humbler the Christian becomes, the more the love of God is aflame in their heart, and vice versa. Therefore, Christian humility is the fruit of knowledge and experience of God's love. On the other hand, the burning love of God in the human heart is insulated by humility so it is liveable and accessible to others. Hence, Pope Francis says, "Without humility, love has no access."

In my years as a member of that Catholic prayer group, I experienced a level of humility born of rare, true love. We called ourselves brothers and sisters. We went to Monasteries and Prayer Mountains to pray. We would often fast, do other spiritual exercises, and then pray for those who requested our prayers. We visited hospitals and homes, and would utilise any opportunity to preach God's word. This made many return to the Church, with some experiencing other conversion forms. We never lacked testimonies of God's interventions in our midst. Various gifts and charisms were common and exercised when needed. Most of us were students, while some were traders; regardless of our backgrounds, we loved and respected each other, were always concerned and reached out when anyone was absent.

Even though we had a leader, a guest wouldn't know who the person was without being told. About Jesus' arrest, remember

Judas was paid not simply to show the Jewish guards where Jesus and his disciples were but also to identify who among them was Jesus, hence the kiss of betrayal. We lived and shared in such a way that an outsider needed to be told who the leader was.

Looking back now to our everyday experiences and all our testimonies and encounters, I now see how humility played a huge role in setting our hearts aflame with God's love and helping us express it without fear of judgement or misunderstanding. Through humility, we abandon ourselves to be led to the fire of God's love, just like gold thrown in fire is purified in the process. As the candle burns away and gives light to the world, so does humility light us up with God's love, so that unhindered by ourselves we can give light to the world around us. Humility does not just insulate the high voltage of God's love; it makes us transparent so the heat and the rays of the fire can pass through us to warm the hearts of those we meet.

Humility and the Healing of Relationships

Humility tells me that I am not, by any means, self-sufficient. I am existentially (if I am honest) in need, often in need of 'the other.' It reveals a divinely purposed incompleteness to be completed by the Other, principally God, and God as manifest in my family, friends, workplace, and all the other places God has planted me (to serve him). Whilst this perceived incompleteness may be hard to accept, it nonetheless serves as a call to the privileged position of being completed by God Himself. In the final analysis, it is an admirable incompleteness.

This is even more so in a marital relationship, where the spouses (husband and wife) are bound together through covenant, such that they, who were two, can now become one, complementing each other for mutual nourishment and fruitfulness.[51] "For the good of the spouses and their offspring as well as of society," Pope Paul VI says, "The existence of the sacred bond no longer depends on human decisions alone. For God Himself is the author of matrimony, endowed as it is with various benefits and purposes."[52] In the knowledge of and faith in this truth, the husband and wife strive daily to live up to the upward calling of their high office whilst submitting to each other. Thus, whilst the wife 'submits' to the husband in love, the husband, in gratitude, gives his whole life for the wife, acknowledging that her life is worth his life. Hence, he would gladly lay down his life for the wife as Christ did for the Church, His bride (Eph. 5:25-26). This relationship between Christ and the Church sets an example of commitment for married couples as a way of living out their lofty vocation of giving one's life to the other frail human person who may not always be able to handle such a precious gift.

However, this union is often strained by human frailty, which often makes a spouse deny their incompleteness without the other. Perhaps, afraid of the reality of this incompleteness, we lie to ourselves and say we are self-sufficient, thinking we don't need the other as much as they need us. Once these false thoughts start to arise, it won't be long before the relationship becomes strained and wounded. And if this endures, then the relationship runs the risk of experiencing a rupture.

The remedy to this is the truth upon which humility grounds us. As I said, humility reveals to us our need for and incompleteness without the other. I said humility does not just consist of knowing who we truly are before God and others. More importantly, it consists of not clinging to what we have come to know or think we know. A scriptural case in point is: "Jesus, even though he was in the form of God, did not count equality as a thing to grasp, but humbled himself." Although Lord and King, Jesus is among us as one who serves.

For a more specific context, let's say that you, as husband or wife, have discovered that you sustain the family financially or otherwise. There is nothing wrong with acknowledging the objective reality that you are the breadwinner. But what is wrong and destructive is clinging to that truth, such that one begins to exaggerate this contribution to the relationship, to the extent of failing to see what the other brings to the table. We become blind to the more profound truth and reality: in our marriage, we are now incomplete without the other. When humility is present, the weaker spouse is treated as the stronger. Ironically, in doing this, the weaker person feels good but, at the same time, sees more clearly, through the lens of charity, the greatness of the lover.

Many marriages falling apart could be significantly attributed to the absence of humility. If everyone clings to their rights and denies their incompleteness, then the assumption of self-sufficiency emerges, thus psychologically isolating each other. Many torn-apart families stand a chance of being healed should humility be brought to the centre of the table and re-contemplated.

Humility and True love

Love is a beautiful thing. It gives meaning and purpose to the human person precisely because we are all creatures of love. Hence, in love we acknowledge our creatureliness and bear witness to our Creator, who is Love in its purest form (see 1 John). While God's love is eternally perfect, ours as human beings is often imperfect and always needs purification, especially at the level of intentions and motivations. If you like, we always need training in the character of love because not everything that appears as love is love, regardless of how the beloved and the lover perceive it.

How strange to find someone in an abusive relationship still considering themselves loved by the abuser! When the supposed lover and beloved aren't firmly grounded in the truth, what isn't love could quickly and successfully pass as love. You would have heard of the expression 'tough love.' Many women suffer dehumanisation and endure inhumane treatments from their spouses, all in the name of tough love. A man abuses his wife or partner and calls it tough love, but gets offended when the woman plays the same tough love game with him. So, what happened to the biblical command, "Do unto others what you would like done to you"? Already, one could see insincerity here. Unfortunately, true love can only thrive in sincerity and truth. Matter-of-factly, we cannot truly love from a false height, and without which the lover cannot appreciably know the beloved. In this case, love can be seen as a mode of knowledge. And without a deep knowledge of each other, the relationship becomes non-flourishing for both spouses.

Since true love has no access from a false height, humility is needed to ground us in the truth of ourselves so we can grasp the truth about our true place, from which alone we can love others. From a false height, love is distorted and loses its very character of self-abasement for the sake of the other in charity. A classic case in point is John 3:16 – "For God so loved the world that he gave his only Begotten Son, Jesus." In the sending of God's only begotten Son, we witness the divine descent for the sake of love.

Furthermore, in his first letter to the Corinthians (13:4-6), St. Paul invites the Christian community in Corinth to live in love. He tells them that love is patient, kind, not jealous nor rude, not boastful nor arrogant. Instead, it bears, believes, hopes, and endures all things—all these we have seen and witnessed in God in their perfect form. However, for our love to be anything like God's, we must deliberately and consciously practise humility to counter the wounded human nature of arrogance, boastfulness, insisting on our ways, etc. True love, an overflow of God's love poured into the human heart (Rm. 5:5), would be impossible without the solid foundation of humility, which grounds us in the truth of ourselves, God, and our neighbours. As it were, it corrects the distortions in our vision.

An Antidote to the Endemic Quest for Domination and Exploitation

If there is something most of us are immediately aware of in our world, especially at a time like ours, it is the endemic quest for dominance and exploitation of the other for ascension to success. As some would say, our world has been so entrenched in this reality that it is becoming the new norm. I am not simply talking about this reality on a global stage, like at the political level. The reality of this quest is also very prevalent at the individual level, where we are often at war with ourselves.

We see and hear of civil unrest, wars, and territorial invasions of countries by others; we see how some states profit from the collapse of other states. When we hear about world peace from our politicians, and more often than not it simply is about the maintenance of the interests of the stronger, those who have what it takes to threaten and control other weak states. Often, when we hear about democracy and human rights, we see many versions of these, each competing for dominance and trying to export and impose its version on the other. But really, what a careful consideration of the matter reveals is the individual states' quest for dominance and control. And to disagree with what is generally accepted but isn't indigenously working for one's own people is tantamount to exclusion, being bullied and punished or sanctioned. As is often the case, the quest for dominance and exploitation blinds and deafens so much that meaningful communication becomes impossible. When the communication of an individual's deep convictions fails, conflict gradually creeps in, sometimes disastrously.

There is a sense in which there is an experience of this even within the Christian faith communities, where everyone is out for their interests rather than having or keeping Jesus' servant-heart at the centre. To achieve this, dominance and exploitation of other people's weaknesses become the order of the day. Undoubtedly, this has contributed to the incidents of abuse we have had in many religious communities.

Considering this insatiable quest for domination and control, one cannot help but ask: Where does all this come from? How are people and systems so insatiable regardless of how much pain their satisfaction can cause to others? This vicious quest comes from a deep-seated wound within us, a situation 1 Timothy 6:5 talks about: "These men regard godlessness as gain." Mark 7:21-23 has it that, "From within one's heart come evil thoughts…theft, murder, adultery, greed, wickedness, deceit, debauchery, envy…all these evils come from within…"

Besieged by this self-poisoning quest, humility becomes that beautiful virtue to think and talk about but not practice. The humiliation that accompanies the virtue of humility is simply unacceptable! This has left us insecure, afraid, anxious, and unhealthily vulnerable, as we deliberately but subtly leverage people's weaknesses for personal ascendance in the short term at the very risk of long term 'dis-ease.' So, when my ascendance becomes the seed of another person's wounds, then Christ's promised peace and joy elude me. Indeed, there is no rest for the wicked. Falsely elevated, one's heart is scarred with deep-seated fear that can never be extinguished without a reach for the truth. In the end, everyone is wounded.

Humility, in this context, provides a healing balm because it invites us to do what a certain homeless young man describes as, "Acknowledge that we are nothing without God." He continued, "Father, humility makes the weak feel strong and good." From my experience, and thinking about what this homeless young man said, I could see how this is true. This is not so much about the façade people put up to appear humble. When one approaches with an authentic, deep-seated sense of humility, heart speaks to heart, deep calls unto deep (Psalm 42:7). All things considered, the other person feels it.

Hence, God's presence doesn't make us feel helpless but empowered, as his presence is a humble presence: "High above the heaven, but he stoops low to the humble of the earth" (138:6). Also, Philippians 2 has it that, "though he was God, he did not count his equality with God a thing to grasp but humbled himself." Such is the brilliance of God's humility and its astonishing beauty when contemplated. Humility also provides sheer strength to bind up wounds and mend broken hearts and mend the breaches, etc. (Isaiah 58:12).

Chapter 9

THE COURAGE AND FIERCENESS OF HUMILITY

Humility as a Sign of Courage

Humility is a sign of strength and courage. To be humble is to reach the core of our being, where we discover our fierceness or how dangerous we are. With this knowledge of self, we learn by grace to contain this power through submission to charity. True humility flows from true knowledge of oneself. Otherwise, it is simply timidity, lack of self-knowledge, or possibly low self-esteem. You cannot really and truthfully self-abase yourself unless you know that you can freely do it, uncompelled. Thus, Jesus said, "I lay down my life; no one took it from me. I laid it down because I have the power to lay it down and to pick it up again" (Jn 10:17). Humility is anything but cowardice.

Only one standing on a false height fears falling. But the one who is firmly grounded is unlikely to be afraid of falling. As such, the fear of falling is experienced only when one stands on a false height, and for which there is an obsessive and destructive determination to keep the said height in order to avoid a fall. Hitherto, the virtue of humility has been trampled upon. There is nothing wrong with being on top of your game or being the best at what you do. After all, God dwells on high, yet his eyes are on the lowly.[53] God could do this because he is humble. Likewise, we, therefore, need humility to ground our feet firmly on the truth, from whence comes courage.

Often, people going through rough patches struggle and are discouraged. As a priest, when the faithful or parishioner approaches me on matters such as this, I first listen carefully to find the root of the discouragement. As is often the case, it comes from one's perceived or experienced reality—I used 'perceived' because often what is perceived to be true can be completely the opposite.

The next stage is to revisit those perceived or experienced realities. Here, the objective is to see how true they are. But most times, the person may need more time to be ready to do this. Sometimes they start with you but eventually become unable to complete this self-scrutiny. The third stage, however, would depend on the outcome of the second stage, which can either be that their perceived reality was indeed true or not. Throughout this process, what we pursue is what I can call the 'ground of truth': *what is, what ought to* and *what ought not to be*. In every Christian's challenge, knowing these three realities or truths provides a firm ground upon which they stand to face life.

However, the realisation of each truth – 'what is, ought to, or ought not' – can sometimes be daunting and challenging. Often, we could be tempted to shy away from or deny the reality of one of these. No matter how ugly or good the outcome of the discernment is, standing on that discerned truth offers more courage than standing or building on presumptuous ground. Do not be afraid or worried because being on the ground, the lowly place of humility, is not a problem for the operation of grace, provided the ground is that of truth, for the Lord raises the lowly and humbles the proud (Prov. 29:23).

True Christian courage stands directly on the solid foundation of truth, which humility helps us attain and accept. If you struggle with the absence of courage, carefully re-evaluate the ground of truth upon which you stand in relation to yourself, others, God, and the world. If they are false, you will always be afraid of falling, and you will always lack the courage of one whose feet are firmly fixed on the solid foundation of humility, which is truth.

The Fierceness of Humility

Humility can easily be associated with many things but hardly with courage and fierceness. Humility is not only courageous but fierce at the same time. First and foremost, we can attest to the truth that it takes courage to be humble and be one's true self in a world where many are becoming conformists to popular views to be accepted or approved. It takes the courage of humility, amid all that, to withstand the increasingly tortuous and unsettling resistance to authenticity and truth in our days, which end up pushing people to embrace the calmness and silence of falsehood, a denial of truth. Humility says, "I cannot pretend to be, nor can I be what I am not, no matter how enticing and incongruous my true self might appear and be frowned upon."

All is by grace and has been received as a gift. I should be a good steward of my true place, ready to give an account of it. Pride renders the Christian a lousy steward who, for fear or many other reasons, abandons their duty post in the absence of their Master. "Blessed is the servant whose Master finds at his duty post when he returns" (Matt 24:46, Lk 12:37). Let us embrace the courage of humility and remain at our respective posts, which is firstly about being our true selves, which pride denies. You are a gift of grace, first to yourself, and then to others. Humility, with a loud and undaunted voice, announces this truth amidst the deafening and tortuous voices of the world to whom we are dead but alive in Christ.

Living Authentically in Hope

The courage of humility helps the Christian hold back from entitlements and accolades, even when they are merited. When this is done for charity and to make Christ manifest, the Christian's life becomes a life lived in anticipation of an eternal reward that surpasses the perishable rewards that the world promises. The tendency to self-gratify through things like revenge, honour, and an undue quest to be approved or proven right, justified, and perfect in the eyes of others is brought under the control of the Holy Spirit, who then becomes our Advocate and the guarantor of our all-surpassing inheritance. He is the one who justifies and approves of us.

In this act of humility, the Christian boldly chooses the lowest place, which is often despised and avoided by many and yet is the place of Christ. Of course, this is not for self-abasement but for lifting others in love. This, indeed, requires courage. Hence, the humble dare to take the true place of Christ among his people, "I am among you as one who serves."[54]

Because of its radical nature and resilience in rising above these basic and vain fruits of pride, humility can often be very fierce in attaining its end, which is the truth. Do not be shocked when I say here that what the world holds against humility isn't just that it appears as weakness and timidity. For some, this might be true.

But for the most part, humility is frowned upon because it upsets the worldly order of things and turns over the tables. It calls the last first and the first last.

More so, humility is detested for its scandalising fierceness, just as the cross remains a scandal to many. It challenges our human senses, which fail at its brilliance and splendour. Contrary to common understanding, humility is courageously fierce. Find a humble person, and you would have found a courageous person.

The fierceness of humility can sometimes manifest as a threat, or at least a suspect, to the proud and ignorant (Wis. 2:12-13).[55] Why? Because it powerfully summons the other to the truth, a journey of descent from the pseudo-heights of false masks and shields.

This process of descent is not without humiliation. You might be shocked to know that I consider humiliation a part of humility, and more so a part of its fierceness. It might also interest you to know that this is not simply my thought, as there exists the scriptural understanding of humility as an experience of humiliation. In Matthew's account of the sermon on the mount, Jesus clearly describes this act of descent as being poor in spirit, gentle, recognising our need for God (hunger and thirst for what is right), showing mercy, having recognised that we still are because of God's mercy, purity of heart, maintaining the bond of peace among us when others are busy showing the stuff they are made of, enduring persecution, abuse, and calumny.[56]

The humble may leave the reward, recompense to the Lord and live with an intense vision of heaven. They embrace humiliation, which accompanies the grace of the truth upon which they now stand. Nobody wants or likes humiliation, but I am so sorry to be the bearer of the bad news that humiliation is part of humility. If humility is only embraced when humiliation is absent, then I am afraid to say that this is not true humility, whose character flows directly from Christ's life, death on the cross, and resurrection. Hence, Pope Francis, in a homily at the Casa Santa Martha chapel, insists that, "Humility is not being polite, courteous, or closing one's eyes in prayer, but being able to accept humiliation." "Humility without humiliation," he says, "is not humility."

In tandem with the above postulations, a humble person would mean someone who, like Jesus, "the Great Humiliated," can endure humiliation for charity's sake[57] Since acceptance isn't the first human instinct in the face of humiliation, authentic humility can be pretty scandalous and threatening to the proud. This is why the humble can be very fierce in dealing with their fears and failures. With unequalled bravery, the humble tries again where they had failed many times. This is because they had already incarnated or are incarnating in him or herself what could be the worst-case scenario, being grounded in the truth and taking the lowest place like Christ. Having taken this place, every event in their life, be it failure or success, leads them closer to the fullness of maturity in Christ.

Ironically, you find that the humble, with their fierce bravery, confront their fears and eventually overcome them. They are not held back by the fear of failure or humiliation. The humble can genuinely say with power, "When there is a casting down, there is a lifting up." This confession has no power or effect in the mouth of the proud, who is standing on a false height that first requires the descent of humility before the lifting up of the spirit can take place. Without the former (humility), the fruits of the latter (the Holy Spirit) are stifled, and we fail to see a lifting up when there is a casting down. Without humility, we fail to see and believe in the power of God to lift the weak. Humility is indeed fierce in its ways.

The Irony and Scandal of Humility

The truth about humility is that it often appears very proud and could sometimes, to a distanced observer, be overpowering. I dare to say that the virtue of humility is very proud of itself as the crown of other virtues. Precisely that which the world frowns at and shies away from, humility prides in and yet remains authentically humble. Since humility is a radical witness to the cross, sometimes it can appear as arrogance because of its truthfulness to itself and others. Grounded in truth, the humble are one with themselves and are not moved so easily. This strength of character can often appear not just as stubbornness but arrogance because humility speaks and acts with the strength and gentleness of the knowledge of the truth.

Do not be shocked when I tell you that the humble are often misunderstood for this reason. Humility's brilliance can be daunting both to the humble and the beholder, although with different effects. To the humble, grace prevents them from knowing their true spiritual state; otherwise, the enemy will tempt them. To a humble observer, it is challenging and seen for what it really is: a lofty but simple spiritual state. To an arrogant observer, it is too good to be true, and they feel condemned. They may look determinedly for opportunities to show where the person lacks the integrity to make themselves feel better. Thus, it becomes an object of doubt and, if you like, a scandal. This is very much true about every virtue in its pure form. Hence, the love manifested on the cross remains a huge object of scandal for many.

Ironically, the voice and acts of the humble do not always come across as very humble, although not for their fault but often due to the distorted perception of the perceiving subject. As spiritual things are spiritually discerned, humble actions are humbly discerned. It would be silly to expect a carnal mind (a mind unaided by grace and the power of the Holy Spirit) to appreciate the spiritual significance of the cross. Only through the Spirit of Jesus could the cross be appreciated. This truth calls us to be careful in our judgement of the actions we call proud and arrogant, as they can often be a sign of our lack of humility.

Being Proud

Being proud of something is in itself a good thing, and even the work of grace. For example, the Christian should be very proud to have known God and been begotten as His child. They should be very proud of God's word. The contrary could be considered pride if they have refused to see their belief in God and His word as a privilege and thus ashamed of Him.

The humble are proud, but proud of being humble and not ashamed to submit to the truth of who they are and have been called to become. The humble are not ashamed to be servants of others and, indeed, don't shy away from being the least.[58] Ultimately, humble people rejoice in their consistent authenticity, constantly striving and refusing to be swayed to walk the path of falsehood or pride.

While it may sound paradoxical to speak of humility as being proud, there is a sense in which authenticity and deep conviction of the truth require one to become very proud. Hence, St. Paul talked about boasting with the cross and not being ashamed of the gospel because it is the power of God for salvation for all who believe (Rm. 1:16, Gal 6:14). Proudly, Jesus announces Himself as the Son of God, who had come to do not His will, but the will of the Father who sent Him. Although He was God, there was nonetheless much confusion as to whether Jesus was a servant and was sent. As a Son, therefore, He spoke openly of His Father. Even when Jesus was called a good teacher, he quickly redirected those praises towards God and said, "Why call me good, for no one is good except God."[59] Even though He was goodness personified, He showed us an example to follow, that all glory and credit should be ascribed unto the Lord.

At the judgement before Pilate, His humility proudly shone forth as He was being humiliated. Then we hear, "Are you a king?" Pilate asks. "You have said so," Jesus replies.[60] Now, this is where it gets even more interesting. In John 19:10, Pilate asks Jesus, "Do you refuse to speak to me? Do you not know I have the authority to release or crucify you?" To some, Jesus' reply here might appear arrogant, but in reality it is both the truth and a manifestation of the brilliance of humility. Jesus, though God, must manifest not His glory but the glory of His Father, God. Pilate talked about his authority to release and crucify, but Jesus will speak about the authority and power of another, upon whom He completely depended on and entrusted His life.

In John 18:36-37, Jesus replies to Pilate, "My kingdom is not of this world; if it were, my servants would fight to prevent my arrest by the Jews. But now my kingdom is not of this realm...For this, I was born." So, clearly, Jesus states the truth: He is a king, but not of this world. He more or less was saying, my kingship is all that you all desire and aspire to be but can't be. Yet I have chosen to leave this authority in the hands of another. Hence, Jesus replies, "You will have no power over me if it were not given to you from above (God)" (Jn 19:11). But how could any sane person choose to declare his kingship in such a pitiable state, without guards, servants, without a crown, practically nothing to show for it? This is the boldness of the truth of humility, not ashamed even when all suggests otherwise.

His sufferings are a deliberate consequence of the descent of the divine to save us. This scene is a direct contrast between divine kingship and worldly kingship, and an invitation to learn humility from Jesus' gentle and humble heart. Nonetheless, Jesus' humility scandalises and confuses so much. The raging voices of the people clamouring for His death and the selfish kingship that intimidated with its authority (*"Do you not know that I have the power to release or crucify you"*) were not enough and could not make the humble Jesus cower or tweak and soften His position. At points like this, the humble must proudly declare and stand for the truth. In Jesus, we clearly see how proud the humble can appear when the truth is threatened, yet always pure, innocent, authentically humble, and self-abasing.

Humility and the Christian Hope

It is not possible, reasonable, nor in the nature of the human person to abase oneself infinitely and without purpose. The self-abasement exemplified in Christ is only possible for the Christian if anchored on the Christian Hope that strengthens humility and gives it meaning and direction. Christian hope empowers the Christian's self-abasement to be ecstatically drawn and directed towards the Transcendent, beyond the created order. Where true Christian humility is found, there Christian hope must be present, and vice versa. In other words, true Christian humility is possible where authentic Christian hope is found.

Thus, the scripture says that because of the joy set before Him, Jesus endured the cross, scorning its shame, and sat down at the right hand of the throne of God.[61] In Jesus' life, we see that humility is not purposeless. Even though it is clearly a descent, this descent is the path to the Christian ascent. However, we must be careful to ensure that an act of humility is not undertaken for a career or any other form of ascension, no matter how pious it might seem. It should indeed be undertaken solely for charity— for love that is not self-seeking.

The experience the descent of humility presents to the Christian can be likened to what the gospel described as the "pruning of the branches so that they may bear much fruit" (see John 15). It can also be likened to what St. Peter calls "a test or trial" (see 1 Peter 1:7). Like gold that is passed through the fire, the descent of humility burns away from the Christian the impurities of falsehood, so that standing on the solid foundation of truth alone, the Christian is elevated and sustained by Christian hope. The constant human process of moving from falsehood to truth can be excruciating, or at least difficult, depending on the depth of falsehood from which the Christian is being pulled.

The Christian, however, is only able to live this experience of humble descent through hope. This is part of the process of Christian redemption, which is offered in hope. The Christian may fail several times in this descent, which, by the way, is their true ascent, but are able to persevere in hope. In his encyclical *Spe Salvi*, Benedict XVI articulates the power of hope in living with the present with all its arduousness. He says, "Redemption is offered to us in the sense that we have been given hope, trustworthy hope, by virtue of which we can face our present: the present, even if it is arduous, can be lived and accepted if it leads towards a goal if we can be sure of this goal, and if this goal is great enough to justify the effort of the journey."[62] Christian hope offers the strength to bear the Christian cross that conforms us more closely to Christ because it bears the seed of purpose and goal, without which true humility is rarely attainable, if at all possible.

However, the hope that is able to do this comes from God. Like humility, God is the source, and precisely through an encounter with God, who is love, do we get connected. St Paul tells us in his letter to the Romans that our hope cannot disappoint because the love of God has been poured into our hearts through the Holy Spirit.[63] St. Paul seems to think that an encounter with the love of God awakens or sows the seed of Christian hope. But this Christian hope is unfailing, not because of human merits but because of what grace has accomplished in Christ Jesus. When this hope is entertained, anchored upon, and lived out through humility, it attains its object in the end.

The Christian Hope offers us the lens through which we see that an apparent descent of humiliation in the eyes of the world is indeed a lifting up, an ascent. Therefore, pray for the renewal of our Christian hope, which strengthens our patience and resolve in times of trial and test through our living experiences.

Humility and the Human *Telos*

While we by grace every day aspire in practice to be as humble as we can, we are very much aware that our humility will always be imperfect here on earth. However, the deeper our humility is (walking in the truth), the greater our freedom and fullness of life in Christ. But there is no need to overthink it. Instead, what is required is daily, constant and deliberate, sometimes only small steps in response to humility's call. Every step or act of humility is a move towards our growth to measure the stature of Christ's fullness.

Humility might be very sacrificial, but its reward by far outweighs its sacrifices. It makes the humble open to the abundance of graces God wants to give each and every one of us. It also prepares the humble for an eternal encounter with our God, who is glorious in majesty but humbly delights in us.

In the final analysis, the human end will be a humble end because, from all our high horses and false heights, we shall be happily humbled, please God, in death because we are meeting Truth. We shall all ascend to the One who is Humility-personified.

Eternal blessedness envisions a perfect spousal union between the believer (the beloved) and God (the Lover) when the latter becomes all in all (1 Corinthians 15:20-28), and all is fully made manifest (Luke 12:2).

We can only imagine what it would be like when God fully manifests in his splendour. Perhaps, like the heavenly hosts, we shall cast our crowns, bowing in humble adoration (Rev. 4:10). Having gazed directly at love face-to-face, the human heart shall be humbled by the Divine Humility that loved it while on earth. It will erupt in it an immeasurable joy and gratitude, which instantly launches them into an eternal, humble but ecstatic descent of complete abandonment in God's awesome presence, simply in adoration.

Instantly, in the One who is One in Himself, we become one with ourselves, against whom we strove to avoid all the while and all through our lives. To its amazement, the soul realises that there is no need to compare itself to another, an undertaking that had triggered an endemic process of "pride" in it. Falsehood vanishes, and only the truth remains; the truth of who we are and have become in Christ. In this state, upon encountering humility in its perfection, our imperfect knowledge and practice of humility give way because it has indeed accomplished its purpose of bringing us home to the fullness of life. We are now one with the One who is truly One and who loves each of us beyond measure. Consequently, the end goal of humility is attained by grace.

REFERENCES

1. Saint Teresa of Avila. The Interior Castle, Chapter 10. In The Complete Works of Saint Teresa of Jesus, edited by E. Allison Peers. New York: Sheed & Ward, 1957, p. 323. ("To be humble is to walk in truth.")

2. Pope Francis. "The Golden Rule of Humility: A Homily Given for the Morning Meditation in the Chapel of the Domus Sanctae Marthae, Monday 8th April 2013." Published by L'Osservatore Romano, weekly edition in English, no. 16, 17 April 2013.

3. Genesis 2:7

4. L. Mezzadri. "Humility in St. Vincent's Apostolic Dynamism." Vincentian Heritage 1 (1981), pp. 3.

5. Constitutions of the Congregation of the Mission (CR) II, 6

6. St. Vincent de Paul's Writings (SV) XI, 54.

7. St. Vincent de Paul's Writings (SV) IX, 674.

8. Maloney, Robert. The Way of Vincent de Paul: Contemporary Spirituality in the Service of the Poor.

9. Mowczko, Margaret. "Meekness." In Discussion on Femininity and Masculinity, 2020.

10. Maloney, Robert. The Way of Vincent de Paul: A Contemporary Spirituality in the Service of the Poor.

11. Philippians 2:6-7

12. Cantalamessa. Sober Intoxication, Volume 1.

13. Pope Francis. "The Golden Rule of Humility: A Homily Given for the Morning Meditation in the Chapel of the Domus Sanctae Marthae, Monday 8th April 2013." Published by L'Osservatore Romano, weekly edition in English, no. 16, 17 April 2013.

14. Maloney, George A., SJ. Entering into the Heart of Jesus: Meditations on the Indwelling Trinity in St. John's Gospel, p. 76.

15. John 14:30

16. Proverbs 13:12

17. Psalm 145:14

18. Matthew 27:46

19. Luke 23:46

20. Luke 1

21. Luke 18:9

22. Romans 3:27

23. Ephesians 2:8-9

24. Isaiah 64:6

25. Isaiah 64:8

26. Luke 7:10

27. John 6:37b

28. John 18:14

29. 1 Corinthians 3:12

30. Matthew 11:29

31. Catechism of the Catholic Church, p. 150.

32. Catechism of the Catholic Church, 143.

33. Psalm 88:18

34. Isaiah 14:13-15

35. Ephesians 4:13-15

36. 1 Corinthians 13:5-7

37. 1 Corinthians 3:1-4, 7

38. Ephesians 4:3

39. Ephesians 4:2

40. Matthew 27:51, Ephesians 2:14

41. Acts 5:41

42. John 3:30

43. Luke 7:28

44. 1 Corinthians 15:28

45. Gambino, Pro. "Discernment: A Christian Way of Life," 18th February 2022.

46. 1 Chronicles 12:32

47. "Pope Francis Teaches Discernment for Coping with Spiritual Battles." National Catholic Reporter (ncronline.org).

48. John 10:9

49. Luke 6:44-45

50. Romans 7:15-25

51. Catechism of the Catholic Church No. 1601, which draws from and explicates Canon Law No. 1055.

52. Gaudium et Spes No. 48.1S

53. Psalm 138:6

54. Luke 22:27

55. Wisdom 2:12 (While this wisdom literature points to the fate and challenges of the righteous (e.g., Jesus) among the wicked, it nonetheless shows that one's submission to God in faithfulness could be very unsettling for those who are proud and wise in their own understanding. The wicked say of the righteous, "He became a reproof to us because his manner of life is unlike that of others")

56. Matthew 5:1-11

57. Pope Francis

58. John 13:1-17. Proudly, Jesus washes the feet of his disciples and remains among them as one who serves. In the Eucharist, Jesus proudly gives himself as food to us, his children.

59. Mark 10:17-18

60. Luke 23:3

61. Hebrews 12:2

62. Benedict XVI. *Spe Salvi*, 2007, p. 1.

63. Romans 5:5

Printed in Great Britain
by Amazon